TEDDY BEARS,
TUPPERWARE
AND
SWEET FANNY
ADAMS

Andrew Sholl

TEDDY BEARS,
TUPPERWARE
AND
SWEET FANNY ADAMS

HOW THE NAMES
BECAME THE WORDS

Michael O'Mara Books Limited

First published in Great Britain in 2013 by
Michael O'Mara Books Limited
9 Lion Yard
Tremadoc Road
London SW4 7NQ

Formerly published as *Bloomers, Biros and Wellington Boots* in 1996, as
The Achilles to Zeppelin of Eponyms in 2000 and as *The Name Game* in 2003
by Michael O'Mara Books Ltd.

A CIP catalogue record for this book is available from the British Library.

Papers used by Michael O'Mara Books Limited are natural, recyclable products
made from wood grown in sustainable forests. The manufacturing processes
conform to the environmental regulations of the country of origin.

ISBN: 978-1-78243-029-2 in hardback print format
ISBN: 978-1-78243-081-0 in EPub format
ISBN: 978-1-78243-082-7 in Mobipocket format

1 2 3 4 5 6 7 8 9 10

Printed and bound by CPI Group (UK) Ltd, Croydon, CR0 4YY

Designed and typeset by K DESIGN, Winscombe, Somerset
Illustrations by Greg Stevenson
Cover design by Anna Morrison

www.mombooks.com

Foreword

What's in a name? From Achilles to Zeppelin, the words and phrases we use every day invoke a whole cast of fascinating historical figures and heroes of ancient myth, but we rarely spare them a moment's thought.

When Captain Boycott made himself so unpopular in Ireland that nobody would do business with him, he could hardly have imagined his name would enter not only the English language but also French, German and Russian!

And when Dr Bowdler and his sister took all the sex out of Shakespeare so that Victorian families could read the bard without blushing, they could not have guessed that for evermore the family name would be associated with absurd prudery.

Behind some everyday names are extraordinary accidents of history. Few, for example, remember the man who invented the Hoover; instead we celebrate a particularly canny marketing man. And, perhaps the greatest irony of all, the origin of the real McCoy, a phrase denoting authenticity, remains hotly disputed to this day.

Whether you're lying back on the davenport in your cardigan, knickerbockers and plimsolls, or sipping a relaxing Martini in the Jacuzzi, you'll discover hundreds of characters we all use in general conversation and the stories that make them so memorable. You've only to turn the page and . . . Bob's your uncle!

Achilles heel

Point of vulnerability. When the oracles foretold of Achilles' bloody end in the Trojan War, his parents went to great lengths to protect their son from his tragic fate. As an infant he was submerged by his mother in the river Styx to make him invulnerable, save for the heel by which he was held. To add to the indignity, he was bundled off to hide in the court of Lycomedes, the king of Skyros, dressed in woman's clothing. It was there that Ulysses found him and entreated Achilles to join the Greek campaign against the Trojans. The valiant warrior was eventually killed by Paris, who fired an arrow into Achilles' one vulnerable spot. **Achillea**, or yarrow, is a genus of aromatic herbs which, according to legend, Achilles used medicinally.

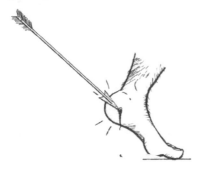

Adam's apple

Protuberance of the thyroid cartilage in a man's throat. Both the Bible and the Koran record the story of the progenitor of mankind created by God from the earth's dust, whose name has since been attached to all manner of objects and activities: **Adam's rib** is a euphemism for woman after the Genesis story of her creation; human toil has been called **Adam's curse** as punishment for eating from the Tree of Knowledge; water is sometimes called **Adam's ale** because it was all the first man would have had to drink. The adam's apple was so named for a piece of the forbidden fruit, which became stuck in Adam's throat.

Adam style

Ornamental style of design. Brothers Robert (1728–92) and James Adam (1732–94) caused a sensation throughout Europe and the US in the 1760s by streamlining the rather severe French neo-classical style, which had dominated interior decoration until then. Their aim, said Robert, was to 'transfuse the beautiful spirit of antiquity with novelty and variety'. The best-known Adam-style furniture was not designed by the Adamses but Thomas Chippendale; their influence was also seen in carpets, silverwork, metalwork and chimney pieces of the time.

Addisonian termination

English essayist and poet Joseph Addison (1672–1719) was a persuasive writer; or, as he would have said, his writing ability was something he was proud of. His practice of ending sentences in prepositions infuriated Anglican Bishop Richard Hurd, who coined the term to describe this reprehensible practice, which still makes English teachers wince. Hurd was perhaps a little harsh; Addison was by no means the only culprit. Addison was a prominent Whig statesman and co-founded the original *Spectator* magazine.

Admirable Crichton

Denoting a person of distinguished ability and all-round talents. James Crichton (1560–85) was a precocious Scottish scholar who mastered foreign tongues, served in the French Army and tutored the young aristocracy in Italy. He was also much admired for his masterful swordsmanship. Alas, he was perhaps too cocky; when Crichton stole away with the mistress of a prince he was set upon by three masked marauders and soon after died from his wounds. The epithet was applied by the Scottish author, Sir Thomas Urquhart. J.M. Barrie's play of the same name tells the story of a particularly able butler who takes charge when his master's family are shipwrecked on a desert island, but reverts to his subservient character when they are later rescued. The play was first performed in 1902.

Adonis

An exceptionally attractive young man. Adonis was a handsome youth adored by the Greek goddess of love Aphrodite. Out hunting in the mountains one day he was killed by a wild boar, presumed to have been another of the goddess's jealous lovers in disguise. The other gods pitied the grieving Aphrodite and transformed the blood of Adonis into a scarlet flower, *Anemone coronaria*, allowing him to spend half the year with her on earth and the other half in the underworld; so the Greeks explained the changing of the seasons and the effect on their crops. The name derives from the Semitic word *adon*, meaning lord, misinterpreted as the name of a Babylonian god. *Adonis* is also a genus of herbaceous plants, which bear red and yellow flowers.

Aesop's fables

Collection of stories in which animals display human characteristics. Different writers give Aesop different origins; he is variously described as a particularly canny slave or a wise traveller who was an attendant at the court of Croesus. Indeed many of the tales ascribed to Aesop date back to ancient Egypt, suggesting that his name may have been invented by the Greeks to give the disparate stories common authorship. Plutarch records that he died at Delphi on a mission from Croesus to distribute a large sum of money. Aesop turned his nose up at the squabbling citizens and deemed them to be unworthy. In response they threw him over a cliff. The first collection of Aesop's fables, now lost, was published in 300 BC; the version we now regard as standard first appeared in Milan around 1480. Scholars have had a difficult time discerning which were the original stories; additional tales have been added throughout the centuries and some have been traced to India.

Albert

Queen Victoria's German husband and first cousin, Albert, the Prince Consort (1819–61), was unpopular in Britain during his lifetime but his status made him something of a trendsetter among fashionable gentlemen. His practice of wearing a watch chain across his waistcoat was much imitated. Only after his death at Windsor was he accorded respect for his tempering influence on Victoria and his restorative effect on the monarchy. Albert's full name was a bit of a mouthful – Francis Albert Augustus Charles

Emmanuel, Prince of Saxe-Coburg-Gotha – so the watch chain became known simply as an Albert.

Alexander technique

Natural therapy relying on correct posture to relieve stress and ensure physical well-being. Tasmanian actor F.M. Alexander (1869–1955) identified the misuse of his voice as the cause of his own chronic laryngitis and spent his life teaching his technique to improve health.

Alice band

Girls' headband worn by the title character in Lewis Carroll's books for children, *Alice's Adventures in Wonderland* (1865) and *Through the Looking-Glass and What Alice Found There* (1871). Illustrator John Tenniel was responsible for the depiction of Alice, including this now-famous accessory. The Alice of the stories was based on Alice Liddell, the second daughter of the dean of Carroll's Oxford college. The tale of the little girl who fell down the rabbit hole was relayed to Alice and her sisters on a boating trip on a hot summer's day in 1862. Carroll, real name Charles Lutwidge Dodgson, was an eminent mathematician. In contrast to the gentle, absurd humour of the stories, he had an unhealthy obsession with young girls, often taking photographs of them in various states of undress.

Alice blue

Shade of blue-green favoured by Alice Roosevelt Longworth, the daughter of US President Theodore Roosevelt. The colour was immortalized in a popular song by Joseph McCarthy, *Alice Blue Gown*.

Alzheimer's disease

A form of premature senility in which patients suffer memory loss and irrationality. Neurologist and psychiatrist Alois Alzheimer (1864–1915) began his studies into the workings of the brain at psychiatric hospitals in Germany and became professor of neurology at Breslau University (now in Poland). He is best remembered for identifying and describing the symptoms of prehensile dementia in 1907. There is no known cure for the disease but new drugs are proving effective in slowing down the symptoms.

Amazon

An unusually tall or physically powerful woman, derived from the ancient Greek *a mazos*, meaning 'without breast'. The mythical race of female warriors from either Scythia or Africa removed the right breast so it would not impede the drawing of a bow. Men from the community were either killed or banished. The tribe is mentioned in the chronicles of the Trojan War.

Amish

Puritanical followers of the Swiss religious elder Jakob Amman (*c*. 1645 to *c*. 1730), who split the Mennonite church in the 1690s. Members of the sect, who had dispersed throughout Europe, began emigrating to the US in 1720 to escape religious persecution and groups are still found in some states of the union and Canada. Conspicuous by their frugality, the Amish spurn modern conveniences such as electricity and lead a simple, rural lifestyle. They speak an antiquated German dialect erroneously dubbed 'Pennsylvania Dutch'.

Ammonia

A pungent, colourless gas. The ancient Egyptians believed the crystalline salt, ammonium chloride, and the gum produced by certain plants possessed medicinal qualities. Both could be found in Libya near the temple of Ammon or Amon, the Egyptian king of the gods. He was represented in art with the head of a ram and equates with the Greek Zeus and the Roman Jupiter. Amon's name translates as 'the hidden one'. The gas in its pure form is used chiefly in fertilizers and is perhaps best known today as an ingredient in household cleaning fluids.

Ampere

Unit measuring the flow of an electrical current, abbreviated to 'amp' and represented by the symbol 'A'. French mathematician André Marie Ampère (1775–1836) sat transfixed as he watched a public demonstration of Oersted's discovery that a wire connected to a battery could influence the direction of a compass needle. He calculated a formula for the force of an electric current and conducted his own experiments to prove his theory. Ampère showed that two wires connected to an electric current attracted and repelled one another – just like a magnet. His work helped prepare the way for Faraday's discovery of a way to transform electrical energy into mechanical energy.

Anderson shelter

Partly prefabricated air-raid shelters first issued in Britain at the outset of World War II, when Sir John Anderson (1882–1958), later Viscount Waverley, was Home Secretary. Anderson was a senior civil servant in the Colonial Office and one-time governor of Bengal before entering politics in 1938; he was elevated to the ministry almost immediately. The small curved steel shelters were erected in back gardens, partly buried and covered with soil, to withstand the impact of shelling. Three million were built throughout the country by war's end. Their designer, Scottish engineer William Paterson, was later knighted for his role in helping to save civilian lives.

Andromeda

Northern constellation of stars two million light years from the earth. When the queen of Ethiopia boasted that her daughter, Andromeda, was more beautiful than the sea nymphs who escorted Poseidon, the angry deities demanded retribution. A sea monster was summoned to destroy the country and Andromeda was offered as a sacrifice by her fearful family. She was rescued by Perseus in the nick of time. The **Andromeda strain** is a term applied to unidentified bacteria that has the potential to destroy mankind, from the 1969 Michael Crichton novel of the same name about a killer virus from outer space.

Anemone

Genus of herbaceous plants that bear large-bloomed, long-stemmed flowers. It is said that the name is a corruption of Nemesis, the goddess of vengeance and retribution, and derives from *anemos*, the Greek word for wind. The flowers, found throughout Europe and the Mediterranean, were introduced to Britain by the Romans and were especially popular in the seventeenth century. Legend tells that Adonis, the young lover of Aphrodite, was transformed into a red variety.

Angstrom

Unit of length used to measure light waves. Swedish chemist Anders Jonas Ångström (1814–74) pioneered the science of spectrum analysis, or spectroscopy, which allows us to determine the make-up of any substance by examining the rainbow of light it emits. He saw that each colour corresponded with a different element and that light waves could tell us which chemical elements were present in the stars. Turning his attention to solar physics, Ångström discovered the presence of hydrogen in the atmosphere of the sun. His discoveries were little known outside Sweden until the 1870s, when he was appointed a Fellow of the Royal Society. The symbol for the angstrom is 'Å'.

Annie Oakley

US slang for a free ticket or a meal ticket, recalling the American sharpshooter, Annie Oakley, originally Phoebe Annie Oakley Moses (1860–1926), who astounded audiences by perforating holes in airborne playing cards among other feats. Complimentary tickets are commonly punched with a hole to prevent them being exchanged for cash; meal tickets and railway tickets were similarly clipped. Annie Oakley and her husband were regulars on the US vaudeville circuit before beginning a seventeen-year association with Buffalo Bill's Wild West Show.

Anthony Eden

Stiff felt hat with a curled brim and a ribbon band, also called a homburg. It was originally made in the Prussian spa town of the same name whose patrons included the Prince of Wales, later to become Edward VII. At the turn of the century, the homburg usurped the top hat as the headgear of fashionable men about town. The black variety earned the nickname, the 'Anthony Eden' in the 1930s, after the dapper, long-serving Foreign Secretary. The fashion was adopted by Eden's political rivals and aspiring dandies at a time when the bowler was an almost mandatory Whitehall accessory. Robert Anthony Eden, later 1st Earl of Avon, followed Winston Churchill as Prime Minister but resigned following the controversial Anglo-French invasion of the Suez Canal in 1956.

Aphrodisiac

Drug or other substance that heightens sexual desire. Aphrodite was the Greek goddess of love and beauty. Mythology records that she originated in the sea near Cyprus (the Greek *aphros* means foam). She is identified with the Roman Venus.

Arachnid

The scientific definition of a class of insects with four pairs of legs, including spiders and scorpions. Arachne was a skilful weaver in Asia Minor who challenged the goddess of wisdom Athena (the Roman Minerva) to a spinning competition. When Athena destroyed her web in spite she killed herself. The piteous goddess turned Arachne into a spider.

Archimedes' principle

Mathematical theory that states the loss of weight of a body immersed in a fluid is equal to the weight that the fluid has displaced. A delicate matter weighed on the head of Hieron II, the tyrannical king of Syracuse – quite literally. He suspected his crown was not made of pure gold and called on Archimedes (287–212 BC) to settle the question. The renowned mathematician and philosopher racked his brain for a solution but retired to a public bath, defeated. As he lowered his bulk into the pool he observed that some of the water had spilled over the sides. Archimedes uttered the now-famous cry, 'Eureka!', and ran home naked, excited by his discovery. Testing his theory on the crown and an equivalent mass of gold, he lowered both into water and gauged the equivalent volume displaced. Archimedes proved the king right: the crown was a phoney. He is also credited with inventing **Archimedes' screw**, the first spiral device for drawing up water from one level to another; the first armour-plated ship, covered by a mesh of iron chains; and for devising the idea for a steam-powered cannon. Archimedes was killed in the sack of the city by the Romans.

Assassin

Fanatical murderer. The original assassins, or *hashishin*, were eleventh-century disciples of the Persian sheik Hassan ben Sabah and so named for their reputed practice of eating hashish before setting out on their murderous escapades against their Turkish rulers.

Atlas

A collection of geographical maps. Atlas was an uncle of Zeus who was condemned to hold the universe on his back for eternity as punishment for his part in the War of the Titans. His image first appeared on Mercator's book of maps in 1595, hence the modern definition.

Aubrey holes

The fifty-six pits which surround the outside of Stonehenge were named in 1959 after the first man to identify them, the Wiltshire antiquary, author and failed lawyer John Aubrey (1626–97), who also uncovered the region's other great megalithic structure at Avebury in 1649. Aubrey's extravagant lifestyle and legal problems forced him eventually to sell all his inherited estates but he gratefully accepted his lot and the charity of friends such as Hobbes and Ashmole. 'If ever I had been good for anything, 'twould have been a painter,' he remarked without rancour late in life.

Audubon Society

The National Audubon Society of the US and Canada is devoted to the protection of birds. It was founded in 1886 in honour of John James Audubon (1785–1851), a naturalist and artist who painted all known species of birds in North America. The illegitimate son of a French naval officer and planter in Santo Domingo (now Haiti), Audubon initially could find no American publisher. His works were instead engraved in England in 1827. Audubon created something of a stir in fashionable London society, appearing in public dressed as a backwoodsman.

Augean stables

Pertaining to a major accomplishment; reforming a corrupt institution. Hercules, the strong son of Zeus, was ordered to perform twelve tasks in punishment for slaying his wife and children. The fifth command involved cleaning out the stables of Augeas, the King of Elis, which contained 3,000 oxen and had not been touched for thirty years. Augeas promised Hercules one tenth of his stock if he could accomplish this feat, which he duly did by diverting two rivers through the stables. When Augeas refused to acknowledge his debt, Hercules later killed the ungrateful king.

August

The eighth month. The greatest achievements of the Roman emperor Augustus (63 BC–AD 14), previously Gaius Julius Caesar Octavianus, fell in the month of Sextilis, the sixth month of the old republican year which began in March. It was renamed in his honour in 8 BC. Augustus was Julius Caesar's nephew and heir. On Caesar's death, he returned from his studies in Greece aged nineteen to take the helm, at first as part of a triumvirate with Lepidus and Mark Antony but he later assumed dictatorial control. Augustus was regarded as a virtuous ruler but one who was as ruthless and as cunning as his opponents.

Avogadro's law

At the same temperature and pressure, equal quantities of gas contain an equal number of molecules. The hypothesis of Count Amedeo Avogadro (1776–1856), a professor of physics at the University of Turin, led scientists to determine the molecular constitution of gases and the weight of atoms. Like many bright ideas, his theory of 1811 lay neglected for more than fifty years.

Babbitt

Unimaginitive businessman. From the title character of the 1922 novel by Sinclair Lewis. George F. Babbitt was a conformist Midwest real-estate agent with little imagination or flair.

Babble

Incoherent speech, gibberish. From the Genesis story of the citizens of Babel (Hebrew for 'the city of God') who suffered pride and sought to build a tower to reach heaven. God punished them by confounding their language.

Bacchanalia

Drunken festivities. The revelries honouring the Greek god of wine, Bacchus (also called Dionysus), grew so outrageous that

they were banned by the Senate in 186 BC. Originally, the festival was a sacred ritual celebrated by women for three days each year. However, some bright spark, it was said with divine inspiration, started inviting men. It was soon transformed into a scandalous monthly orgy.

Drunken orgiastic behaviour is also sometimes described as 'dionysian'. Bacchus's Roman equivalent is Liber (*see* **libation**).

Baedeker

These German guidebooks that provided practical advice to the nineteenth-century traveller were intended to save him the cost of hiring a guide. The publishing house of the same name was founded in 1827 by Karl Baedeker (1801–59). The books also initiated the system of rating accommodation and places of interest with stars. Air attacks on English cities by the German Luftwaffe in 1942 in retaliation for Allied sorties against German targets were nicknamed **Baedeker raids**.

Bailey bridge

Portable military bridges, constructed from lightweight steel sections and capable of rapid erection. British Ministry of Supply engineer Donald Coleman Bailey (1901–85) first demonstrated their capabilities in 1940; the bridges were quickly introduced thereafter to aid the war effort. Bailey bridges helped the Allies make rapid advances into north-west Africa and north-eastern Europe. Bailey was knighted for his services at the end of the war.

Bakelite

The first thermosetting plastic, a synthetic resin that does not melt under heat, was invented by Belgian-born US chemist Leo Baekeland (1863–1944) in 1908. Three years earlier he had set out to find a synthetic equivalent to shellac, a resin that could be dissolved back into its original state. Instead he stumbled upon a combination of phenol and formaldehyde that was to pave the way for the modern plastics industry. Uses for the product were many: telephones, wireless sets and automobile parts to name a few. It did not make Baekeland his first fortune. He had previously invented Velox, the world's first commercially viable photographic film. George Eastman of Kodak fame bought the rights in 1899 for $1 million.

Baker days

Extra training days for British teachers were introduced by the Conservative Education Secretary Kenneth Wilfred Baker (1934–) in 1987 as part of a package of reforms to raise teaching standards and ultimately to benefit pupils. The immediate effect however, was that students had extra time off school. Baker held the post from 1986 to 1989 and latterly has devoted his time to literary pursuits including a volume on the history of political cartoons and collections of verse. His autobiography was titled *The Turbulent Years* (1993).

Balaclava

Woolen garment covering the head and neck that was worn by soldiers at the Battle of Balaclava in 1854 during the bitter cold of the Crimean War. Balaclava was the site of the ill-fated Charge of the Light Brigade. Lord Raglan gave a muddled order to the brigade to disrupt the Russian cavalry. But instead of riding towards the retreating troops on the heights, the brigade led by Lord Cardigan charged straight into Tennyson's 'valley of death' below. Nearly half of Cardigan's men were killed. Years later, the Poet Laureate evened the score, penning a verse to commemorate the more successful Charge of the Heavy Light Brigade in the same battle.

Banksia

Genus of trees and shrubs with spiky flowers found in Australia and Papua New Guinea, named after Sir Joseph Banks (1743–1820). 'Any blockhead can go to Italy!' declared the amateur botanist, passing up the fashionable continental Grand Tours of the day for the chance to accompany Captain Cook on his voyage of discovery to the southern hemisphere in 1768. The son of a wealthy Lincolnshire family, Banks could afford to hire a personal tutor to teach him the rudimentaries of botany. His journeys, accompanied by artists, assistants and hounds, garnered many plants that were then unknown and won Banks instant celebrity and the firm friendship of King George III. Banks was elected president of the Royal Society in 1778, a position that he held until his death forty-two years later. His influence was also felt in the decision to transport convicts halfway round the world; Banks strongly advocated Australia as the ideal location for the new prison colony rather than the other destinations under consideration, Gibraltar and the west coast of Africa.

Banting

Dieting. A portly London undertaker and cabinet-maker William Banting (1797–1878) was an early disciple of the weight-loss programme. His doctor prescribed a diet free of carbohydrates, and for twelve months fatty foods and alcohol did not pass his lips. The results were impressive: Banting had lost 46 pounds and published his slimming secrets in a tract called *Corpulence* (1864).

Bartlett pear

See Williams pear

Baud rate

Unit measuring the number of data transmissions in computer systems or teleprinters. One baud or unit pulse equals the rate of one bit (or binary digit) of information per second. French engineer Jean-Maurice-Emile Baudot (1845–1903) succeeded in speeding up the rate of telegraphic transmissions in 1874. Unlike Morse's time-consuming system of dots and dashes, Baudot's language was based on permutations of electrical pulses allowing each five-digit code for each letter to be transmitted simultaneously.

Bawbee

Halfpenny or copper coins, originally a Scottish coin from the reign of James V. The name is thought to derive from the title of the mint-master of the day, the Laird of Sillabawby, Alexander Orok. One bawbee was equivalent to three and subsequently six Scottish pennies, and could be exchanged for an English halfpenny. The coins, made from a silver base, were first minted in 1541.

Beau Brummell

A fop. George Bryan Brummell (1778–1840) had the gift of the gab but frittered away his many opportunities. At Eton he so impressed the Prince of Wales (later George IV) that he was offered a position in the regent's own regiment. Retiring from the military after a relatively short time, he then inherited a family fortune, setting up house in fashionable Mayfair and cultivating a reputation as the most stylish gent in all England. The newly crowned king, it was said, 'began to blubber when told that Brummel did not like the cut of his coat'. But the king tired of his friend's biting wit. Mounting gambling debts forced Brummell into exile in Calais and then a French prison cell. As Brummel's mind grew increasingly feeble he would host parties for imaginary guests. He died in Caen in an asylum.

Beaufort scale

A scale which measures the force of wind at sea, originally defined as the effect of wind on a full-rigged man-o'-war. The measurements, from zero, equalling calm conditions, to eleven, signifying a storm, were devised by Commander Francis Beaufort (1774-1857) and adopted by the Royal Navy in 1838. The system became the mandatory international standard in 1874. A further six classifications for hurricanes were added in 1955.

Béchamel sauce

Simple white sauce consisting of flour, butter and milk or cream. A French general and nobleman at the court of Louis XIV, Marquis de Béchamel, is credited with inventing the recipe. A similar sauce, the velouté, meaning 'like velvet', uses stock instead of milk.

Becquerel (Bq)

Unit of radioactivity, named after French physicist Antoine Henri Becquerel (1852–1908), who discovered the phenomenon. He shared the 1903 Nobel Prize for physics with Pierre and Marie Curie (*see* **curie**). In 1895 Becquerel placed a quantity of uranium salts on a photographic plate to test whether phosphorescent materials emitted X-rays. He discovered that a power source other than ordinary light had penetrated the photographic paper, confirming the presence of radiation. Minute quantities of radiation are measured in becquerels; larger amounts in curies.

Bedlam

Pandemonium or a busy, crowded state of affairs. A contraction of the Hospital of St Mary of Bethlehem in London, founded in the thirteenth century and which became a lunatic asylum in the fourteenth century. Upon its transfer to Moorfield in 1676 the hospital was a popular tourist attraction as Londoners flocked to ogle the lunatics.

Begonia

Genus of herbaceous plants that bear fragrant pink or white flowers named in honour of statesman and scientific patron, Michael Begon (1683–1710). Begon was the administrator of France's American protectorates, including Canada and the French West Indies. The territories were progressively ceded to the British after France's military defeats of the eighteenth century.

Behemoth

Object of massive proportions. Biblical animal described in the Book of Job as having bones as strong as brass and a tail as big as a cedar. The beast was so big that it was kept in the desert lest it drank the contents of the river Jordan in one gulp. It is thought to have been a hippopotamus or an elephant and corresponds with the aquatic leviathan.

Belcher

Blue neckerchief or handkerchief with white spots popularized by English boxer James 'Jem' Belcher (1781–1811) and now taken to mean any handkerchief. In 1803, Belcher lost an eye in a fight and retired from the ring to run a pub.

Belisha beacon

Flashing amber light mounted atop a black-and-white striped pole at pedestrian crossings, introduced in 1934 when Isaac Leslie Hore-Belisha (1893–1957), later 1st Baron Hore-Belisha, was Minister for Transport. Belisha's road-traffic bill sought to cut the mounting death toll on the nation's roads. Provisions were made for more pedestrian crossings, and driving tests and a comprehensive highway code were introduced. His career ended sensationally at the War Office in 1940 after one fight too many with Army chiefs. Belisha had repeatedly warned about the weakness of defences in France. Four months after his resignation the lines were breached by German forces.

Benedict Arnold

US euphemism for traitor. Connecticut volunteer soldier Benedict Arnold (1741–1801) fought valiantly in the American War of Independence, leading the ill-fated attempt to capture Quebec for the rebels and the successful attack on the British fleet in New York. The public hailed Arnold as a hero but his brash ways were not welcomed by his colleagues and he was repeatedly passed over for promotion. Feeling slighted, Arnold secretly negotiated with the British before being exposed as a spy. He evaded capture and death by hanging and lived out his final ignominious years in England.

Benedictine

Brandy and herb liquer originally distilled by Benedictine monks. Benedict of Nursia (*c.* 480 to *c.* 547) dictated the rules for monastic life in the Middle Ages, pronouncing that monks should be employed in manual labour, impart knowledge to youth and live orderly, obedient lives. Benedict had settled for a hermit's existence while still a boy but his guidance was widely sought and he was appointed the abbot of a monastery at Vicovaro. The lack of discipline accelerated his departure and Benedict founded a monastery based on his own beliefs at Monte Cassino, near Naples. Members of the order are sometimes called 'black monks' from the colour of their habit. In 1964 Benedict was anointed the patron saint of Europe by Pope Paul VI.

Bernoulli effect

Scientific principle at the heart of aerodynamics, which states that the faster a fluid moves, the lower the pressure. Hence air travels faster over the top of a curved aeroplane wing than underneath and allows the vehicle to lift into the air. Swiss scientist Daniel Bernoulli (1700–82) was a member of a distinguished family of mathematicians, famous for their rivalry. When he and his father were jointly awarded a prize for astronomy, the elder Bernoulli asked his son to leave the house, insisting the honour should have been his alone. Bernoulli's theorem appeared in *Hydrodynamica* in 1738.

Berserk

Wild, frenzied manner. In Norse mythology, Berserk was a fearless warrior who fought in a savage frenzy, spurning armour and wearing only a bearskin coat (*ber* = bear + *serkr* = coat).

A subsequent legend arose in the eighth century of a Scandanavian hero Berserker who refused to wear iron mail and emulated the god's behaviour on the battle field.

Bessemer process

Working independently of one another, Sir Henry Bessemer (1813–98), the Hertfordshire engineer, and a US scientist William Kelly, invented a process for mass-producing steel from cast iron. It involved blasting air onto the molten iron, which oxidized the carbon, removed impurities and produced a metal better able to withstand stress. Iron from the furnace was poured into a **Bessemer converter**, a large steel vessel with holes at the bottom through which the air was blown. A prolific inventor, Bessemer numbered among his other creations an early hand-cranked machine gun and a gold-coloured powder made from brass for use in paint. He was knighted in 1879 and was bestowed with many honours and awards.

Big Ben

Strictly speaking, the name applies solely to the thirteen-and-a-half ton hour bell installed in the Clock Tower at the Houses of Parliament; more commonly it refers to the tower itself. It was named for Sir Benjamin Hall (1802–1867), later Baron Llandover, the Commissioner of Works when the original sixteen-and-a-half ton bell was cast in 1856. The following year a four-foot-long crack appeared and the bell had to be recast, losing three tons in the process. Hall's own great feat was the establishment of the metropolitan board of works and the substantial renovation of London's parks. He championed the right of Welsh churchgoers to attend services in their own language and campaigned against the mismanagement of ecclesiastical properties. The nickname was also popularly applied to a noted pugilist, Benjamin Caunt, who retired from the ring in 1857, aged forty-two. The four-quarter bells and the hour bell rang out for the first time in 1859.

Big Bertha

German gun of large bore capable of bombarding Paris during World War I from well within German lines, up to seventy-five miles away. Employees at the Krupp Works in Essen rather unsportingly dubbed the weapon *dicke Bertha* or 'fat Bertha', after the owner of the factory, Bertha Krupp von Bohlen und Halbach (1886–1957), the great-granddaughter of the company's founder. The family ordnance and manufacturing business was broken up by the Allies after World War II.

Billy-o

With great enthusiasm. The expression is considered most likely to be a euphemism for the devil but a procession of historical figures may also deserve some credit. Nino Biglio was one of the Redshirts fighting for the unification of Italy in 1860 alongside Garibaldi, and the feisty seventeenth-century rector Joseph Billio was expelled from the church for his non-confirmist beliefs. The phrase 'puffing like billy-o' rose to prominence when William Hedley's early steam locomotive Puffing Billy was catching the public imagination.

Biro

László Bíró (1900–85), a Hungarian journalist, sought a pen with quick-drying ink and hit upon the idea of using a small steel ball to control the flow. He registered his first patent in 1943 after fleeing from the Germans, first to France then to Argentina. The Royal Airforce immediately saw the potential of the new pens that did not leak or smudge at high altitudes. The British Government quickly bought the wartime rights to the invention. The civilian version went on sale in 1945 but Bíró neglected one small detail – to patent his idea in the US where expensive copies were marketed as underwater writing instruments. On their first day of sale, New Yorkers bought 10,000 of the then expensive pens. Production of cheaper, disposable ballpoints was developed in 1953 by France's Marcel Bich. A prototype ballpoint pen was developed in the US by John H. Lond in the 1880s.

Blondin

High-tensile wire supporting cable cars; a tightrope. The high-wire act performed by French acrobat Charles Blondin or Blondini, real name Jean François Gravelet (1824–97), attracted worldwide notoriety, particularly his repeated crossings of Niagara Falls. He made his first successful attempt in 1859 and placed increasingly difficult obstacles in his path to maintain the public's interest: performing the feat wearing a blindfold, on stilts, carrying another person on his back. Blondin continued to perform his acrobatic feats until old age forced him to retire. He settled in England and died aged seventy-three.

Bloody Mary

Cocktail containing vodka, tomato juice and a dash of chili and Worcestershire Sauce. Mary Tudor (1516–1558), England's last reigning Catholic monarch, was mortified by the break with Rome and the establishment of the Anglican Church by her father, Henry VIII, and its consolidation by her half-brother, Edward VI. On her accession to the throne, Mary restored Catholicism as the state religion and was intolerant of criticism from the landed nobles who had benefited from the sack of the monasteries. Three hundred opponents burned at the stake, including the Archbishop of Canterbury, Thomas Cranmer; many more Protestants hanged. Her zealous campaign coincided with the loss of England's hold over Calais and disloyal subjects denounced their queen as 'Bloody Mary'. Mary died childless. Her niece, Elizabeth I, undid her work and re-established the Church of England.

Bloomers

Baggy women's undergarment; originally an entire costume with loose trousers gathered at the ankle. Amelia Jenks Bloomer (1818–94) was a New York postmistress whose championing of

women's rights included their mode of dress. The outfit, designed by Mrs Elizabeth Miller, the daughter of a New York congressman, and introduced in 1894, was not a success and the innovation was much derided. Previously, Bloomer was a big draw as a stump speaker and published a magazine, *Lily*, to propagate her views on feminism and temperance.

Bluchers

Heavy half-boots. In the initial stages of the Battle of Waterloo, Wellington's army was strong enough only to hold back a wave of French assaults. The appearance on the battlefield of the Prussian troops, led by the seventy-three-year-old Field Marshal Gebberd Leberecht von Blücher (1742–1819), sealed the victory. It was a defining moment for the old soldier, who had once been drummed out of the cavalry for insubordination.

Bluebeard

Murderous husband. In the old European folk tale, Bluebeard sets off on a journey, leaving his new bride with the keys to the castle and specific instructions to stay away from one room. Curious, she unlocks the door, only to reveal the remains of Bluebeard's previous wives. On his return, Bluebeard finds a bloodspot on the keys and his wife's disobedience is revealed. She too is about to be killed when either she, her brothers or a handsome page slays the villain. The story was widely popularized by Charles Perrault in his book *Contes du Temps* (1697) and the epithet has been applied throughout history to figures including Henry VIII and Gilles de Rais (1404–40), a French nobleman who fought alongside Joan of Arc and slaughtered more than 140 children.

Blurb

Details printed on the jacket of a book; advertising jargon. Originated in a 1907 book by US humourist Gelett Burgess, which featured a shapely young woman called Miss Belinda Blurb.

Bob's your uncle

Everything is all right. Of uncertain origin, but this phrase entered the vernacular in the 1880s when Arthur James Balfour was making his meteoric rise through the ranks of Lord Salisbury's Conservative government. Salisbury saw in the young man great promise and appointed him Chief Secretary to Ireland, then First Lord of the Treasury and finally, in 1902, Salisbury stood aside and handed Balfour the Prime Ministership. Of course, it might have helped that Robert Arthur Talbot Gascoyne-Cecil (1830–1903), 3rd Marquess of Salisbury, was Balfour's uncle. Nothing is a problem, wags would remark, when 'Bob's your uncle'.

Bobby

British policeman. Tory politician and statesman Sir Robert Peel (1788–1850) has the singular distinction of bequeathing both his first and last names to the one profession. Early in his political career Peel was appointed Chief Secretary for Ireland and, under an administration that refused calls for Catholic emancipation, introduced the Irish constabulary to maintain civil order. It was during this period that the term **peeler** was first used to describe police officers. Peel's efficient administration led to rapid promotion and the Home Secretaryship, when he established the world's first modern police force in 1829. Thus 'Bobby's boys' or 'bobbies' entered the vernacular. During a period of political upheaval for the Tories, Peel became Prime Minister, repealing the Corn Laws that severely restricted imports and allowing some concessions to Irish Catholics. He also laid the foundations for the modern Conservative Party. Both terms in fact pre-date Peel. Bobby the Beadle once signified those authorized to secure appearances in the court or church and, similarly, bobbies used to enforce university rules at Oxford. But the meaning applied to the word 'peeler' has changed completely; in the sixteenth century it was an expression for a thief.

Bo Derek

Wall Street slang for bonds that matured in 2010. Popularized during the run of the 1979 film, *10*, even though the character played by the American actress was classified as an '11' by her lustful suitor!

Bode's law

Formula calculating the distance between the planets and the sun, discovered by German astronomer Johann Daniel Titius in 1766 and propagated by the director of the Berlin Observatory, Johann Elert Bode (1742–1826). Also known as Titius-Bode's Rule.

Boolean algebra

The mathematics of logic, basic to the design of computer circuits. Englishman George Boole (1815–1864) pared algebra down to its most rudimentary: any problem, he observed, could be solved by choosing either to proceed in one direction or another. Therefore the right answer lay in the right combination of just two digits, 0 and 1. The same binary principle applies today when programming a computer; tasks are performed by switching electric circuits either on or off. The personal computer in the study, the country's telephone network and spacecraft controlled by NASA all operate on principles conjured up in the abstruse mind of the professor of mathematics and logic at Queen's College Cork . . . in 1847. Boole tried to construct a mechanical device to demonstrate his system, a task not achieved until 1879 when

Sir William Thompson (later Baron Kelvin) built an analogue machine capable of solving finite equations. Boole married Mary Everest, the niece of the geographer whose name was given to the highest mountain in the world. One of the couple's daughters, Lucy, became the first woman chemistry professor in England.

Bosey, bosie

Australian cricketing colloquialism for the style of trick bowling known also as the googly. England player Bernard James Tindal Bosanquet (1877–1936) was its inventor. During World War II the term was applied to a lone bomb dropped from an aeroplane.

Botticelli

Beautiful woman, after the shapely females rendered by Florentine artist Sandro Botticelli (1445–1570), originally Alessandro di Mariano Filiperi. While Botticelli lived in relative obscurity, since the nineteenth century his paintings, particularly *The Birth of Venus*, have come to typify our conception of the Renaissance. However flatteringly it is applied, the name roughly translates from the Italian as 'little barrel'.

Bougainvillea

Genus of shrubs and small trees native to the tropical and subtropical Mediterranean. French navigator of renown Louis Antoine de Bougainville (1729–1811) commanded the first French naval expedition round the world. He charted the South Pacific and claimed Tahiti and other island territories during the three-year voyage. He might well have stumbled upon Australia had not the coral expanse of the Great Barrier Reef forced him to turn back north. He later played a role in the American Revolution, sought to colonize the Falkland Islands and was ultimately rewarded by Napoleon, who appointed him a senator. One of the Solomon Islands was named Bougainville in his honour.

Bowdlerize

To censor or sanitize written material in the style of Edinburgh physician Dr Thomas Bowdler (1754–1825). The editor of the notorious *Family Shakespeare* in 1818 and the revised version of Edward Gibbon's *Decline and Fall of the Roman Empire* promised to omit words and expressions 'which cannot without propriety be read aloud in a family'. Bowdler was much criticized but his work had the desired effect of reintroducing classic works to a prudish Victorian audience. There is also evidence to suggest the original bowdlerizer was not the doctor but his sister, Henrietta Maria Bowdler, who is said to have been responsible for the first, unsigned edition of *The Family Shakespeare*, published in Bath in 1807.

Bowie knife

Long, curved hunting knife popularized by the hero of the Alamo, Colonel Jim Bowie (1796–1836). The first Bowie knife was fashioned by a Louisiana blacksmith from a design by Bowie's brother, Rezin. Bowie, a plantation owner and politician, used it with remarkable success in an infamous duel in which six people were killed, forcing him to flee the state. The knife was sent on to Philadelphia where copies were marketed under his name. Bowie ended up in Texas, where he joined the movement for independence from Mexico. The stand-off resulted in the battle at the famous fort, in which Bowie, Davy Crockett and their supporters were killed.

Bowler hat

Felt hat with a rounded crown and narrow curled brim, named after Thomas and William Beaulieu or Bowler, two Southwark feltmakers involved in its production. Once the regulation headgear of the city gent, the bowler was intended to be worn in the countryside. A nineteenth-century Norfolk squire, William Coke, asked hatters James Lock & Co., to come up with something which wouldn't catch on branches overhead when out shooting or riding. The bowler was a familiar sight in the working man's wardrobe from the 1860s onwards and became the essential accessory for fashionable businessman after World War I. Its connections with the business world led to the term **golden bowler**, to signify a lump sum paid to officers on their discharge from the military.

Boycott

To withhold relations on account of differences, collective ostracism. A bad harvest hit the estates managed by retired British Army captain, Charles Cunningham Boycott (1832–97), in County Mayo, in Ireland. When the captain refused a request from tenant farmers to lower the rent by a quarter he became the focus of a campaign by nationalist leader Charles Stewart Parnell, who urged the tenants to refuse all communication with those who would not meet their demands. Boycott had to seek help from the army to harvest the crops and left Ireland indignant the following year. The word 'boycott' has entered other languages; for example, *boycotter* in French, *boycottiren* in German and *boikottirovat* in Russian.

Boyle's law

At a constant temperature a volume of gas is inversely proportional to the pressure. The Anglo-Irish chemist Robert Boyle (1627–91) announced his theory in 1662, which was also discovered independently by a French physician Edme Mariotte fourteen years later. Boyle rejected Aristotle's belief that everything was made up of either earth, fire, wind or water, and instead declared that matter was composed of elemental particles. His work on the properties of gases led to the modern theory of chemical elements. A founding member of the Royal Society, Boyle was also a noted writer; one essay is said to have inspired Jonathan Swift to write *Gulliver's Travels*.

Bradshaw

Train timetable. Engraver and printer George Bradshaw (1801–53) published the first railway guide in 1839 soon after the establishment of Britain's railway network. *Bradshaw's Railway Companion* and its familiar yellow supplement, *Bradshaw's Monthly Railway Guide*, which appeared two years later, were published continuously until 1961. Bradshaw was a devout Quaker whose philanthropic ventures included helping to establish schools for poor children. He was abroad on business when he died of cholera and his remains were buried in the grounds of a cathedral in Christiania, in Norway.

Braggadocio

A cowardly boaster, with 'lofty looks hiding in a humble mind'. The vain and lustful poet Braggadocio appeared in Edmund Spenser's (1552–99) allegorical tale of the court of Gloriana, *The Faerie Queen*. Gloriana was said to be based on

Elizabeth I; Braggadocio was rumoured to be one of her many suitors, François, Duc d'Alençon (1554–84), the son of Henry II of France.

Braille

The written language composed of raised dots that enable the blind to read and write was devised in 1829 by Louis Braille (1809–52). The Parisian educator was himself blinded at the age of three as a result of an accident in his father's harness workshop. Braille refined a similar, more rudimentary system invented by a French army captain, Charles Barbier, which allowed military messages to be read in darkness.

Bramley apple

Green cooking apple that is one of the most popular varieties in Britain. Bramley Seedlings, to give them their full name, first came to the public's attention when they were observed growing in the garden of Matthew Bramley, a butcher at Southwell, Nottinghamshire, in the 1850s. In fact, they had been cultivated as early as 1809 by Mary Ann Brailsford, the previous owner of the cottage and orchard. The original Bramley tree was toppled in a severe storm at the beginning of the twentieth century but a new branch sprouted, which produces apples to this day. Bramleys are tart when eaten raw, but be patient, they sweeten around Easter.

Bright's disease

Dropsy. In 1827 a physician at Guy's Hospital in London, Richard Bright (1759–1858), discovered that the swelling of the body, a condition known as dropsy, was caused by an inflammation of the kidneys and the infection of the organ's blood vessels. Bright's disease, now known as nephritis, usually occurs after a streptococcal throat infection. Bright travelled widely throughout Europe, not limiting his journeys to sightseeing. On a visit to Brussels in 1815 he delayed his return home to attend to casualties of the Battle of Waterloo. Bright collaborated on a medical textbook with Thomas Addison and was appointed Queen Victoria's physician on her accession to the throne in 1837.

Brobdingnagian

Huge, enormous. The race of giants ruled by a selfish king in Jonathan Swift's satire, *Gulliver's Travels* (1726).

Brock's benefit

Intense argument. C.T. Brock manufactured the colourful fireworks used in the annual display at London's Crystal Palace between 1865 and 1936. Nowadays the phrase is rarely used except when there is a particularly fiery parliamentary debate, which is referred to as a 'real Brock's benefit'.

Bromelia

Tropical plants with jagged leaves of the genus Bromel. They are indigenous to South America and the West Indies and take their name from Swedish botanist Olaf Bromelius (1639–1705).

Brougham carriage

The first four-wheeled carriage designed to be pulled by only one horse was invented in 1838 by Scotsman Henry Peter Brougham, later 1st Baron Brougham and Vaux (1778–1868). Brougham was a notable lawyer who famously defended Queen Caroline against the annulment order sought by King George IV. As a prominent Whig politician Brougham advocated an end to slavery and for textbooks to be available to the working classes at an affordable price; he rose to become lord chancellor under the administrations of Earl Grey and Lord Melbourne. The coach featured an open driver's seat at the front but was otherwise closed. It was so small – it could seat three passengers, and then only at a stretch – that Brougham described his invention as 'a garden chair on wheels'.

Browning rifle

Magazine-fed weapon that doubles as a light machine gun and is capable of firing six hundred and fifty rounds per minute. When inventor John Moses Browning (1855–1926) introduced the firearm in 1918 it was adopted straight away by the US Army and remained in service until the 1950s. Browning built his first weapons as a teenager in his father's Utah gun shop. He was responsible for many innovative developments: he designed the first pistol with a recoil spring mounted in a slide above the barrel. Many of his designs for sporting rifles and machine guns were taken up by other arms manufacturers, including Winchester and Colt.

Brumby

Wild horse. English-born Major William Brumby bred horses in New South Wales in the early nineteenth century. However, many escaped and ran wild. Alternatively, the term may derive from *booramby*, an aboriginal word meaning wild.

Bunkum

Spoken nonsense. Derived from Buncombe County, the North Carolina home of Congressman Felix Walker who made a particularly windy address to the House of Representatives in 1820. In response to catcalls from his colleagues, Walker is said to have remarked, 'I am not speaking for your ears. I am only talking for Buncombe'. The phrase 'talking for Buncombe' was eagerly picked up and given to mean any speech that was especially nonsensical. The phrase also spawned the abbreviations **bunk** and **hokum**, a combination of hocus and bunkum.

Bunsen burner

Gas burner used in laboratories, consisting of a metal tube with an adjustable air valve and a gas inlet. The simple object was introduced in 1855 by the German chemist Robert Wilhelm Bunsen (1811–99), who was also to help discover the chemical elements rubidium and caesium. The long-serving professor of chemistry at Heidelberg University carried out important work on the composition of gases but banned the study of organic chemistry in his laboratory when an experiment went wrong and he partially lost sight in one eye. The unlucky Bunsen also discovered a cure for arsenic poisoning but nearly died of it himself while working with a highly toxic compound which contained the element.

Burton, gone for a

Missing without trace or prior warning. Popularized during World War II, the phrase came to be associated with the disappearance of airmen. It is purported to originate with an advertising campaign for Burton's Ales but there are other plausible associations with a chain of High Street gentlemen's outfitters, Montague Burton. Pool halls situated above the shops were used as RAF medical centres; also measurement for a suit may have come to signify measuring for a coffin. Alternatively, the origin of the phrase may rest with the town of Burton-on-Trent, rhyming slang for 'went'.

Butskellism

That rare instance in British politics when parties on both sides of the political divide agree on a common approach to policy. The term coined by the *Economist* refers to the post-war Chancellors of the Exchequer, Conservative R.A. Butler (1902–82) and future Labour leader Hugh Gaitskell (1906–63), both of whose economic policies embraced a combination of planning and market freedom.

Butterick patterns

Standardized paper patterns for clothing were introduced in 1859 by Massachusetts tailor Ebenezer Butterick (1826–1903). As demand soared, Butterick established factories in Fitchburg, Massachusetts, and later moved his operations to Brooklyn, New York. He also founded a fashion magazine, *Metropolitan*, to promote pattern sales.

Cadmium

Metallic chemical element, symbol Cd, atomic number 48. In Greek mythology, Cadmus was the founder of Thebes and the originator of the Greek alphabet. Founding the city was no easy task: he first had to slay a dragon and then a number of warriors who had sprung from the beast's teeth. The term **Cadmean victory**, meaning a victory won with significant loss, was once as common a term as the synonymous Pyrrhic victory. Cadmium is commonly found in control rods for nuclear reactors and is used in the manufacture of electroplating.

Caesar

Julius Caesar (100–44 BC) traced his origins back to one of the most venerable Roman families and to ancient Etruria. The name came to imply 'reigning emperor' and was adopted by his immediate successors. It lives on today in the imperial German **kaiser** and the pre-revolutionary Russian adaptations **czar** or **tsar**. Lesser mortals, particularly in the US, are sometimes granted the epithet by the press to imply their elevated status; for example, a senior health official may be referred to as a 'drugs czar', a police chief as a 'crime czar'. Julius Caesar also gives his name to the **caesarian section**, the extraction of a baby by cutting the mother's abdomen and womb. This was the supposed method by which Caesar or the progenitor of his family was born. Alternatively, it may simply be derived from *caesus*, the past participle of the Latin word meaning 'to cut'.

Caesar salad

Tossed assemblage of lettuce, garlic-flavoured croutons and Parmesan cheese, mixed with olive oil, lemon juice and a dash of Worcestershire sauce. In 1924, on a particularly busy night at his Tijuana restaurant, owner Caesar Cardini famously improvised the recipe from the ingredients at hand. The argument rages in culinary circles, of course, about the place of the anchovy in the Caesar salad. It made its first appearance (and many have said it should have been the last) courtesy of 'Prince' Mike Romanoff, a Hollywood restaurateur.

Calliope

Steam-driven keyboard instrument from the nineteenth century commonly associated with the circus and named after the Greek goddess of lyric poetry. Calliope, whose name means 'beautifully voiced', was one of the nine Muses and is said to have been the mother of the poet Orpheus, who was able to charm hideous monsters with the music of his lyre.

Calypso

Musical style originating in nineteenth-century Trinidad among black slaves, the lyrics of which contain topical themes. In Greek myth, Calypso tended to the shipwrecked Ulysses and held him for ten years on the island of Ogygia. She bore him two sons and promised to make him immortal but Calypso could not convince Ulysses that this was where he belonged. Only when the gods interceded (either Athena or Hermes) was Ulysses allowed finally to return to Ithaca.

Camellia

Genus of flowering shrubs and trees native to India and Indonesia, including tea. George Kamel (1661–1706) was a Moravian Jesuit and botanist who travelled throughout Asia. Japanese women traditionally use the seeds from another species as a source of hair oil.

Cant

Hypocrisy. The word has its origin in the Latin *cantus*, 'to sing', and by the sixteenth century was being used to describe the whining tone of beggars. Yet the myth subsequently grew that cant, meaning to imply false piety, was connected to the Scottish minister, Andrew Cant (*c.* 1590–1663). Perhaps there is some truth to the story. In the 1630s, Cant was an eloquent critic of plans by Charles I to introduce an English-style church to Scotland. By 1641 he was preaching before the king at Edinburgh and during Cromwell's Commonwealth so passionately defended the monarchy from the pulpit that English soldiers in the congregation drew their swords.

Cardigan

Knitted woollen waistcoat first worn by British soldiers to protect themselves against extreme cold during the Crimean War. The garment was introduced by James Thomas Brudenell, 7th Earl of Cardigan (1797–1868), who reputedly paid £10,000 from his own pocket each year to ensure his was the most smartly dressed regiment in the British Army. On a mistaken order from Lord Raglan, Cardigan's men rushed directly towards Russian artillery positions in the famous Charge of the Light Brigade in 1854. One third were killed. The battleground at Balaklava also gave its name to the woollen garment covering the head and neck, the **Balaclava** (*sic*) **helmet**.

Cartesian

System of philosophy promulgated by the French mathematician and thinker René Descartes (1596–1650) which holds that nothing is real unless it can be proven as such. Self-belief was the starting point of his doctrine, summed up by the famous aphorism: *cogito ergo sum*, 'I think, therefore I am.' Descartes' controversial beliefs and his attempts to prove the existence of God contributed to his decision to move from Amsterdam, where he spent much of his working life, to Sweden and the court of Queen Christina. However, within five months of his arrival he died of pneumonia.

Casanova

Promiscuous lover, philanderer. The notorious Venetian adventurer and novelist Giovanni Giacomo Casanova de Seingalt (1725–98) travelled throughout Europe upon his expulsion from a seminary for scandalous conduct. Casanova moved in the highest circles and was many times decorated. He purportedly worked as a diplomat, a spy for Louis XV, escaped from prison in Venice where he was serving a sentence for sorcery, and counted Catherine the Great among his amorous conquests. His reputation as a notorious libertine is largely garnered from his unreliable *Mémoires écrits par lui-même*, published in twelve volumes between 1828 and 1838. Casanova escaped his numerous creditors and lived out his final days as a librarian for a Bohemian benefactor.

Cassandra

Prophet of doom. Cassandra was the daughter of Priam, the king of Troy, and was given the gift of prophecy. But when she refused the advances of Apollo, the god placed a curse on her, ensuring her accurate prophecies were never believed. In vain Cassandra foretold the fall of Troy to the Greeks.

Catherine wheel

Spinning firework, sideways somersault. When the emperor Maxentius asked for her hand in marriage, the virgin St Catherine of Alexandria declined, protesting she was already 'married to Christ'. The angry ruler ordered Catherine's torture on a spiked wheel but the bonds broke as soon as it began to turn. She was beheaded shortly after and milk, not blood, flowed from the wound. According to legend, angels transported her body to Mount Sinai, where her supposed relics still lie in a monastery. The cult of St Catherine was enormously popular in the Middle Ages. Ironically, she became the patron saint of wheelwrights and spinners; the miraculous flow of milk from her severed head led to her adoption as the patron saint of nurses.

Celsius

Centigrade thermometer scale. Swedish astronomer Anders Celsius (1701–44) devised a scale to standardize thermometers in 1742. He decreed the temperature at which water freezes to be zero degrees and its boiling point, one hundred degrees. A similar principle had already been established in 1730 by Frenchman René Antoine Ferchault de Réaumur, but the glory and eventually the nomenclature went to the Swede. Celsius was the professor of astronomy at Uppsala and built the town's observatory.

Chartreuse

Venerated French liqueur made from a combination of brandy and herbs; a shade of green resembling the most recognizable variety of the drink. Monks from the ascetic Carthusian Order first distilled the distinctive green and yellow varieties at a monastery outside Paris in the seventeenth century. Since 1835 they have been commercially available from the Grand Chartreuse, near Grenoble, where the order was founded by St Bruno in 1040.

Chateaubriand steak

Thick fillet steak, garnished with herbs. The term originally applied to the method of preparation, grilled and topped with Béarnaise sauce. It was devised in 1822 by Montmireil, the personal chef to François René, Vicomte de Chateaubriand (1768–1848), when the statesman and writer was the French ambassador to London. He was no stranger to the city where, a quarter of a century earlier, he had spent seven poverty-stricken years in exile during the French revolution. It was also where Chateaubriand wrote his best-known work, *Génie du Christianisme* (1802), an impassioned defence of the Catholic Church.

Chauvinism

Intolerance of others; excessive patriotism. Nicolas Chauvin typified the old French soldier who had fought for the glory of the Revolution and the Empire. He was much decorated for bravery on the battlefield but his bellicose patriotism and worship of Napoleon made him a figure of ridicule. Chauvin began to appear as a character in drama, which only cemented his reputation for preposterousness. The meaning of the word evolved gradually and is now commonly employed as a slight against men who are either too proud or too inconsiderate to take into account the feelings of women, as in **male chauvinism**.

Chesterfield

Comfortable, upholstered sofa with arms and back at the same height. Philip Dormer Stanhope, 4th Earl of Chesterfield (1694–1773) first bequeathed his name to a long overcoat with a velvet collar, fashionable in the eighteenth century. The well-padded sofa came along one hundred years later and may well be connected with the Derbyshire town of the same name. Chesterfield was a parliamentarian whose wit exceeded his statesmanship; the famous letters to his illegitimate son and godson offered frank advice on how to get ahead in society and earned their author a reputation for being a callous cynic. His most eloquent critic was Samuel Johnson, who complained he had been neglected by his patron when most in need of patronage.

Chippendale

The Gentleman and Cabinet Maker's Director (1784), the most comprehensive book of furniture designs of the eighteenth century, established Thomas Chippendale's (1718–79) reputation as England's finest furniture maker. The son of a Yorkshire carpenter, Chippendale established a London workshop where he designed and constructed drawing-room furniture based on the fashionable rococo and neo-classical styles. Chippendale's son, Thomas junior (1749–1822), rescued the firm from the brink of bankruptcy to create some of the best regency-style furniture. Whereas Chippendale was once a byword for quality, it is better known today as the name of a troupe of risqué male dancers and two cartoon chipmunks, Chip 'n' Dale.

Clarence

Large four-wheeled carriage for four passengers, containing seats facing one another. The clarence was introduced in the first half of the nineteenth century and named after the Hanoverian William Henry, the Duke of Clarence (1765–1837), who ruled as William IV from 1830. The carriage was also sometimes known as a 'growler' for the noise it made and a 'crawler' for its pace. As monarch, William was anxious to maintain the power of the

Crown over Parliament and only grudgingly accepted reform. He was a scandalous figure, siring ten illegitimate children by the Irish actress, Dorothea Jordan.

Clementine

Citrus fruit, *Citrus reticulata*, thought to be a hybrid of the bitter orange and the tangerine but similar to the mandarin in flavour. It was first produced in Algeria *c.* 1900 by Père Clément, a French priest, and the name was formally adopted two years later by French horticultural authorities. It is grown throughout the Mediterranean.

Clerihew

Satirical verse of two rhyming couplets of uneven length, usually about an eminent person. Writer Edmund Clerihew Bentley (1875–1956) wrote his first humorous poem in 1890 to amuse friends at St Paul's School in London, among them G.K. Chesterton. It read:

> Sir Humphry Davy
> Detested Gravy.
> He lived in the odium
> Of having discovered sodium.

His inaugural collection, *Biography for Beginners* (1905) was published under the pseudonym E. Clerihew, his mother's maiden name. The name stuck and the style was widely admired and much imitated by poets including W.H. Auden. Bentley also published detective stories and was a venerable Fleet Street leader writer. The humorist, Nicolas Bentley, said of his father: 'it gave him more pleasure than anything else he achieved in life that he lived to see the word "clerihew" . . . enshrined in the Oxford Dictionary as part of our language'. (*see* **Davy lamp**)

Cocker, according to

Exactly, correctly. London engraver and teacher Edward Cocker (1631–75) reputedly penned *Arithmetick* (1678), a mathematical text published posthumously. The book was a notable success, running to 112 editions and its accuracy gave rise to the famous expression, first delivered in *The Apprentice* (1756), a farce by Irish playwright Arthur Murphy. However, it is reputed that the works published after Cocker's death had been forged by his editor and publisher, John Hawkins.

Colossal

Enormous. The legend arose that the bronze statue of Helios, the Greek god of the sun, bestrode the entrance to the harbour at Rhodes, but there is no hard evidence to support the claim. The Colossus, Greek for 'larger than life', was completed by Chares in 280 BC. It was said to have been more than one hundred feet high and was regarded as one of the Seven Wonders of the Ancient World. The giant statue was toppled by an earthquake half a century later in 224 BC. Colossus was the name given to the first reliable computer; it came online in 1943 and was used to crack German cipher codes.

Colt

The 'six shooter' handgun revered in the legends of the American West and adopted as the standard service revolver by the US military. Connecticut firearms manufacturer Samuel Colt (1814–62) ran away to sea in his teens and, according to a dubious story, based the design of the mechanically revolving cylinder on a ship's wheel. Colt put early financial woes behind him in 1847 when the US Army placed an order for one thousand pistols for use in the Mexican War. The six-shot, .45-calibre revolver was introduced by the company eleven years after its founder's death and, despite a brief break in production in the twentieth century, remains in production today. In 1905, John Tagliaferro Thompson, the inventor of the Tommy gun (*see* **Tommy gun**), conducted extensive tests on the handgun, establishing .45 as the standard calibre for military use.

Columbine

Prostitute; flower. In Italian *commedia dell'arte* and, later, English pantomime, Columbine was the servant girl who was mistress to Harlequin and the daughter of Pantaloon. In Italian, the affectionate term *columbina* refers to a woman who is as 'gentle as a dove'. The word also refers to colourful, five-petalled flowers of the genus *Aquilegia*, found in North America and Europe.

Condom

Male contraceptive sheath. The sexual renaissance in the Europe of the eighteenth century meant an increasing incidence of veneral disease. A certain Englishman, variously a doctor or a guards officer called Condom or Condum, was said to have popularized the practice of wearing animal intestines knotted at one end. Exports of the contraceptive device apparently boomed; Louis XV ordered them in the hundreds. The name may also derive from the French town of Condom, south-east of Bordeaux.

In fact, condoms had been in use since the sixteenth century and were endorsed by early safe-sex advocates like the Italian anatomist Gabrielle Falloppio (*see* **fallopian tubes**). Rubber condoms replaced sheep gut in 1840 and the latex variety, still in use, originated after World War I.

Coulomb

Unit of electric charge, defined as the quantity of electricity conveyed in one second by the current of one ampere. The aristocratic French physicist, Charles Augustin de Coulomb (1736–1806), broadened our understanding of electricity and magnetism, defining the force with which like electrical charges repel and opposites attract, known as Coulomb's law. Coulomb's genius was not enough to stop his expulsion with other nobles from Paris during the French Revolution but he was able to return in 1795 to continue his research and again take public office.

Cox's orange pippin

Britain's most popular dessert apple was first grown by retired brewer Richard Cox at Slough, Buckinghamshire, in 1825. It is believed to derive from the French Ribston pippin, first brought to Yorkshire from Rouen in 1707. Initially the variety was not resistant to diseases and did not find favour with growers until the introduction of spraying in the 1920s. More than 100,000 tons of Cox's are harvested each year in the UK alone. The words 'pippin' and 'pips' derive from the Old French *pépin*, originally meaning any apples grown from seeds.

Crap

Excreta, to excrete; nonsense. Thomas Crapper constructed the standard flushing toilet in 1886, inventing the U-bend that improved sanitation. However, the word 'crappe' entered the English language as far back as the fifteenth century from the Dutch *krappen*, meaning to separate or cut off, and the Old French *crappe*, defined as grain trodden under foot and mixed with dirt. The connection with bodily functions appears to be directly linked to Crapper; the latter definition being first recorded in the late nineteenth century. A prototype water closet was invented in 1589 by Sir John Harrington.

Creutzfeldt-Jakob disease

Fatal virus affecting the brain that leads to the rapid onset of dementia. German physicians Hans Creutzfeld, (1885–1964) and Alfons Jakob (1881–1931) described the symptoms of this disorder which, like bovine spongiform encephalopathy (BSE or 'mad cow disease') and scrapie in sheep, is caused by the presence in the brain of an abnormal protein. Most humans with the complaint die within twelve months of diagnosis; there is no known cure. There is growing concern that there may be a link between eating beef and contracting CJD but evidence is inconclusive. Injecting material from infected animals or people, such as human growth hormone given to children, is the only proven method of transmission. A rapid rise in the number of cases in Britain may be attributable to increased surveillance.

Croesus, rich as

The ancient King of Lydia who grew so rich his name became synonymous with great wealth. His fortune helped to pay for the temple of the goddess Artemis at Ephesus, the ruins of which can still be seen in Turkey. Part of the columns and sculpture from the temple are now in the British Museum. Croesus was overthrown by his Persian foe, Cyrus, in 546 BC after fourteen years of rule.

Cruft's

Famous dog show, established in 1891 by salesman Charles Cruft (1852–1939) as a publicity stunt to sell dog biscuits. Cruft was unenthusiastic about joining the family jewellers and instead joined James Spratt, a new company which sought to capitalize on the US craze for 'dog cakes'. His dog shows were run for profit and made Cruft a wealthy man; only after his death did his widow hand over the running of the competition to the Kennel Club. Cruft's was held at Olympia for most of the twentieth century and moved to the National Exhibition Centre in Birmingham in 1991 to accommodate the increasing number of dogs and spectators.

Cupid

Roman god of love. The childlike deity, whose name translates from the Latin as 'desire', is usually depicted with wings and

carrying a bow and a quiver of arrows. In Virgil's *Aeneid*, Venus sends him to fuel the passions of Dido and Aeneas and later Cupid begins his own tortured love affair with the mortal Psyche (*see* **psyche**). In Christian tradition, Cupid was portrayed on coffins as a symbol of life after death, which explains his representation in art and association with cherubs. His Greek equivalent is Eros.

Curie

Unit of radioactivity. 'Madame Curie is very intelligent,' observed Albert Einstein (*see* **Einstein**), 'but she has the soul of a herring.' It was certainly true that the great French physicist, born Marya Sklodowska (1867–1934), had little time for social niceties. She and her scientist husband Pierre (1856–1906) were awarded the Nobel Prize for physics in 1903 for their discovery of two new chemical elements, polonium (after Marie's native Poland) and radium. But the couple claimed they were too busy to attend the prize-giving in Stockholm. Even her husband's death in a road accident three years later did not diminish Madame Curie's scientific endeavour. She took over Pierre's chair at the Sorbonne, holding the distinction of being the first woman to win the Nobel Prize and the first female professor at the university. In 1910 the Nobel committee again honoured Marie with the chemistry prize for her work in isolating pure radium. She inevitably died of leukemia, brought about by overexposure to radiation. The artificially produced chemical element, **curium** (Cm), atomic number 96, was named in the Curies' honour.

Cyrillic alphabet

Writing system for Slavic languages, used in Russia and other Eastern European countries. In the ninth century, Rostislav, the ruler of Moravia, asked the Pope to send missionaries to teach the Scriptures in the local tongue. Two Greek brothers, St Cyril, originally Constantine, (*c.* 827–69) and St Methodius (*c.* 825–84), developed an alphabet based on Greek and Hebrew characters, containing forty-three letters. A long-running fight ensued with the German Church, which also claimed the territory and demanded the exclusive use of the Latin liturgy. Cyril became a monk but Methodius, confirmed as archbishop, was imprisoned and tortured by the German Church until the Pontiff's intervention could secure his release. The alphabet has been modified somewhat since Cyril's time and modern-day Russian contains thirty characters.

Daguerreotype

The most reliable of the early forms of photography. In 1829, painter Louis-Jacques-Mandé Daguerre (1789–1851) teamed up with the physicist Joseph-Nicéphore Niépce, who had produced the first French photograph. Until then, methods were crude and development was a time-consuming process taking up to eight hours. Their new process involved coating a copper plate with silver bromide and exposing it to the light. Daguerre continued with his experiments after Niépce's death in 1833 and in 1839 finally perfected the daguerreotype. Exposure now took a matter of minutes and photography became commercially viable. Daguerre was awarded the Legion d'Honneur.

Dahlia

Genus of herbaceous plants native to Central America and grown for their distinctive flowers. The Spanish conquistadors brought back the Dahlia from the New World and presented the first specimens to the Abbé Cavanilles, the curator at Madrid's botanical gardens. He named the flower in honour of his friend and sometime associate, Andreas Dahl (1751–89), a noted Swedish botanist and former pupil of Linnaeus. The Abbé distributed the new plant throughout Europe; the French considered the tuber a delicacy, at least until they tried eating it. The bitter taste confirmed that the new plant belonged in the garden, not on the plate.

Damocles, sword of

Sign of impending danger. The faithful retainer of the Roman god of wine, Dionysus, endured torment at a banquet when a sword was hung over his head, suspended by a hair.

Darby and Joan

The quintessential loving couple made their first appearance in a ballad by printer and councilman Henry Woodfall, *The Joys of Love never forgot*, published in the *Gentleman's Magazine* in 1735. Their relationship is summed up in the third verse:

> Old Darby, with Joan by his side,
> You've often regarded with wonder.
> He's dropsical, she is sore-eyed,
> Yet they're never happy asunder.

In the twentieth century the term came to be applied to homosexual couples and became rhyming slang for the telephone. The author had been apprenticed to a John Darby (d. 1730) of Bartholemew Close, in the pocket of London known as Little Britain (so called because it once housed the Dukes of Brittany). Woodfall was the father of William 'Memory' Woodfall, a parliamentary reporter who could memorize whole debates that he would later transcribe.

Darwinism

Evolutionary theory proposed by the naturalist Charles Robert Darwin (1809–82). The epic voyage of HMS *Beagle* opened Darwin's eyes to the idea of the survival of the fittest. He was struck by the varieties of species on the Galapagos Islands which did not exist on the mainland and discovered the fossilized remains of creatures which were long since extinct. Darwin's first foray into print was an essay in 1844, the circulation of which was limited to friends and a select number of colleagues. But other scientists were beginning to come to the same conclusions and Darwin hastened the publication of his famous tome, *The Origin of Species by Means of Natural Selection or the Preservation of Favoured Races in the Struggle for Life* (1859). The book created an immediate sensation and the survival of the fittest was hotly debated by the scientific community and the Church. Its sequel, *The Descent of Man and Selection in Relation to Sex* (1871) was no less controversial for linking man and the apes, and its conclusions are still contested by some religious groups today.

Davenport

Large upholstered settee; originally a compact writing desk with a sloped top popular in the eighteenth century. The English firm of Gillow sold the first such model to a Captain Davenport.

Davy Crockett hat

Racoon-skin cap, complete with tail, supposedly worn by the 'king of the wild frontier'. Crockett (1786–1836) was a Tennessee backwoodsman whose affable style translated well into politics. He was elected to the state legislature in 1821 and later served in the House of Representatives. His ghost-written autobiography and a number of periodicals exploited his macho image and formed the basis of a successful Walt Disney television programme in the 1950s. Fess Parker's portrayal of the folk hero led to a craze among children for Davy Crockett hats. Crockett's real life adventures ended with Colonel Jim Bowie (*see* **bowie knife**) at the Alamo, when 200 men defending the besieged Texan mission were massacred by 3,000 Mexican troops.

Davy Jones's locker

Eighteenth-century euphemism for a grave at the bottom of the sea for drowned sailors. Possibly a colloquial version of the biblical story of the devil (Davy), Jonah (Jones) and the whale (the locker). There is also a dubious story of a notorious London innkeeper of the same name whose patrons were drugged and spirited away to any ship in need of extra crew members.

Davy lamp

At the conclusion of his triumphant tour of Europe, the coal-mining industry sought the assistance of the great Cornish chemist Sir Humphrey Davy (1778–1829) to solve the problem of underground explosions. He devised an oil lamp enclosed in wire gauze; the gauze deflected the heat, preventing the flame from igniting the gases outside. A gracious Davy showed magnanimity by refusing to patent his invention. The scientist rose to fame as an exponent of the new discipline of electrochemistry. In 1807, using electrolysis, he discovered potassium and chlorine and later isolated other chemical elements. He was also dogged by a persistent young bookbinder's apprentice who had delusions of becoming a scientist himself. When in 1813 Davy fired an indolent assistant, he called for the eager youth. So began the brilliant career of Michael Faraday, the father of electricity. Davy is also the subject of a famous clerihew (*see* **clerihew**).

Decibel

Unit used to quantify sound intensity, identified by the symbol 'dB'. Like the Richter scale that measures earthquakes, decibels are graded on a logarithmic scale. A noise that registers at 3dB in intensity is ten times louder than a noise of 2dB. The units, bels, of which a decibel is a one-tenth measurement, were named in honour of the inventor of the telephone, Scotsman Alexander Graham Bell (1847–1922). After emigrating to the US, Bell was inspired by his work with the deaf to investigate the mechanics of transmitting speech. In 1876, the twenty-eight-year-old Bell and his colleague Thomas Watson invented a device that could carry sound via electrical impulses over a wire. The patent was fiercely contested by other inventors but was upheld by the courts.

Derby

Sporting contest, more specifically a horse race; US name for a bowler hat (*see* **bowler hat**). Edward Smith, 12th Earl of Derby (1752–1834), established two important events on the racing calendar: in 1779 the Oaks, named after his house in Epsom, Surrey, and the following year, the Derby. It is considered the greatest of the classic English races and is contested at Epsom

Downs each year in June. Both colts and fillies run a course a mile and a half in distance and the colts invariably win. The first recorded Derby winner was a horse called Diomed; the celebrated Shergar won by the greatest distance, ten lengths, in 1981. Other race meetings have appropriated the name, most notably the Kentucky Derby in the US. His Lordship scandalized society by marrying a celebrated actress within two months of the death of his first wife. Derby's grandson was to become a Conservative prime minister.

Derrick

Any contraption which hoists heavy weights, such as the steel structure mounted over an oil well to aid in raising and lowering the drill tube; a crane which hoists cargo using a swinging boom. Around 1600 a notorious hangman of the same name carried out his grisly trade at Tyburn, the chief place of execution in London. Tyburn Tree, a euphemism for Derrick's gallows, was located at what is now Marble Arch in the centre of town. Execution day in London was a public holiday so that the masses would reflect on the consequences of wrongdoing; instead public hangings became a spectator sport. Such were its connotations with death, that when the area was settled Tyburn Road was renamed Oxford Street and Tyburn Lane became Park Lane.

Derringer

Small pocket pistol with a large bore, manufactured by Philadelphia gunsmith Henry Deringer (1786–1868) and misspelled by a careless reporter. Abraham Lincoln's assassin, John Wilkes Booth, used a derringer pistol, the size of which allowed for concealment and contributed to its popularity among women. Deringer designed many weapons used by US troops and learnt his trade from his father, who made rifles in colonial Pennsylvania.

Dewar flask

Double-walled glass vacuum container, better known today as the household Thermos flask. The silver-layered internal walls of the vaccum compartment help minimize heat loss. Scottish chemist and physicist James Dewar (1842–1923) became the first scientist to produce liquid hydrogen and devised the vacuum flask in 1872 to help store liquefied gases at extremely low temperatures. He had earlier developed the explosive cordite with fellow chemist Sir Frederick Abel.

Dewey decimal system

Decimal classification system used by most public libraries, devised by New York librarian Melvil Dewey (1851–1931). A library's contents are divided into ten basic groups and specific topics further sub-categorized, allowing for continued expansion. The library at Amherst College in Massachusetts, where as a student Dewey devised his system, was the first to put it into use. He was at one time the director of the New York State Library and founded the American Library Association.

Dickensian

Euphemism for Victorian squalor, a constant theme of the fiction of Charles John Huffman Dickens (1812–70), much of which drew on his own impoverished background. The names of many of the characters contained in Dickens's serialized novels have also become synonymous with the traits that they exhibit, such as Pickwickian (*see* **Pickwickian**). The phrase, 'What the Dickens', refers not to the eminent author but a sixteenth-century nickname for the devil.

Diesel engine

Internal combustion engine, in which compressed air is pumped into the cylinders, producing a temperature high enough to burn the fuel. French-born German inventor Rudolph Diesel (1858–1913) worked as a refrigeration engineer and dreamt of building the perfect 'rational heat motor'. A patent in 1892 attracted the interest of the Krupp Works and under their patronage Diesel produced the first compression-ignition engine five years later. Diesel's machine was twice as efficient as existing steam engines, cheap to build and could run on unrefined fuels. Sadly, it only realized its potential after the death of its inventor. He disappeared, presumed drowned, from a mail steamer en route from Antwerp to Harwich.

Dionysian

see **bacchanalia**

Dixieland

Nickname for the US southern states. Dixes or dixies were US ten-dollar bills issued by the Citizens' Bank of New Orleans in the 1830s. The French word for ten, *dix*, was printed on the reverse. The original phrase 'Dixie's Land' came from a popular minstrel song written by Daniel Decatur Emmett in 1859 that celebrated the 'land of de dixes'. Like many performers who wrote about the south, Emmett was in fact a northerner. The roots of the phrase conceivably go back to 1763, when English surveyors Charles Mason and Jeremiah Dixon charted the demarcation between the southern and northern states.

Dobermann

Powerful dog of German origin with a short, smooth coat, usually black or brown with rust-coloured markings. Louis Dobermann (d. 1884) was a tax collector and keeper of a dog pound in the town of Apolda, Thüringen, who sought an agile companion to accompany him on his duties. The new breed was based on the German pinscher and originally much smaller than today's specimens. The first Dobermann in Britain was called Harras and was imported from Germany in 1911.

Doily

Ornamental mat now invariably made of paper. Mr Doyley or Doyly's drapery stood on the Strand for 150 years from the reign of Queen Anne. His name, probably French in origin, was first applied to a 'cheap and genteel' woven woollen fabric. Addison writes of his 'Doily suit', another eighteenth-century writer tells of a newly impoverished family whose 'children were reduced from rich silks to Doily stuffs'. Jonathan Swift records in his journal of 1711 'coarse Doiley-napkins, fringed at each end, upon the table to drink with'.

Dolby

Trademark noise-reduction system for stereo units and cinema audio, which employs electrical circuits to eliminate tape hiss during the recording process. By 1965, the London laboratories of US engineer Ray Milton Dolby (1933–) were marketing noise-reduction technology to recording studios. The Dolby B system, which eliminates hiss on cassette tapes, was introduced six years later. The name is so zealously guarded that the company took musician and producer Thomas Dolby (real name Thomas Robertson) to court for breach of copyright. The case was settled when the performer agreed to license the name.

Don Juan

Licentious lover, a rake. The debauched fourteenth-century nobleman Don Juan Tenorio earned his place in history's rogues' gallery, thanks to a morality play, *El burlador della Sevilla* (1630), written by the prolific Spanish dramatist Gabriel Téllez, writing as Tirso de Molina. In the original version, the notorious libertine seduces an innocent girl, murders her vengeful father and mocks him by taking a statue of the dead man to dinner. The statue, possessed by ghostly forces, draws Don Juan into hell. The drama inspired Mozart to pen his opera *Don Giovanni* (1787) and works by writers such as Byron, Balzac and Shaw.

Doubting Thomas

A sceptic. In the Book of John, the apostle Thomas refuses to believe his colleagues' reports of Christ's ressurrection until he is shown tangible proof: 'Except I shall see in his hands the nails, and put my finger into the print of the nails, and thrust my hand into his side, I will not believe.' Jesus reappears and rebukes his disciple for his doubt. The incident is used to convey Christ's accessibility to all Christians. Apocryphal stories tell of Thomas's journey to India, where he spread the Gospel and was martyred.

Doulton ware

Decorative pottery produced by Doulton & Company in Staffordshire. John Doulton (1793–1873) established his pottery works in London in 1815, providing pipes for plumbing and other sanitaryware. But when students at the nearby Lambeth School of Art started decorating brown stoneware vessels produced by Doulton the company was inspired to create its own line of painted porcelain, establishing a new factory in Staffordshire and engaging teams of talented artists for this purpose. King Edward VII granted the company permission to market its products as Royal Doulton in 1901.

Dow-Jones index

Average of US stock and bond prices first compiled in 1884 by Dow Jones & Company, a financial news service owned by journalist Charles Henry Dow (1851–1902) and his partner Edward D. Jones (1856–1920). The company started out delivering daily news updates to Wall Street's banks and brokerages. Two years later the flimsy newsletter became the venerable *Wall Street Journal* and Dow its founding editor.

Draconian

Extremely severe. It fell upon Draco, the chief magistrate in Athens, to draw up the city's first written criminal code. The result, produced in 621 BC, was rather drastic. Almost every crime was punishable by death.

Dunce

Slow-witted person, idiot. Medieval scholar John Duns Scotus (*c.* 1265–1308) was the most inspired opponent of the rationalism advocated by Thomas Aquinas, who had sought to establish a distinction between reason and faith. But after his death, the followers of Scotus, known as Scotists or Dunsmen, were ridiculed for their steadfast refusal to countenance any theological reform. Steadily, the name of their brilliant Scottish mentor came to signify any person dim enough to oppose progress and, as a consequence, stupidity in general.

Earl Grey tea

A blend of teas (usually Assam and Ceylon), scented with the peel of the bergamot or substitute. It reputedly acquired its name when a consignment was forwarded to Charles Grey, 2nd Earl Grey (1764–1845), by a Chinese dignitary grateful for the intervention of a British diplomat who had saved his life. It was soon produced commercially and remains a popular premium blend. A prominent Whig, Grey campaigned for Catholic emancipation. As prime minister (1830–4) he presided over the passage of the Reform Act of 1832, enfranchizing middle-class voters, and the following year abolished the last vestiges of slavery throughout the British Empire.

Echidna

Small egg-laying mammal native to Australia and Papua New Guinea, also known as the spiny anteater. This strange creature of the family Tachyglossidae was considered, like the platypus, to be so improbable that naturalists named it after a ferocious Greek monster with a woman's body and a serpent's tail. Echidna devoured passersby, and counted the dragons guarding the Golden Fleece and the Sphinx among her horrible offspring. She also makes an appearance in Edmund Spenser's *The Faerie Queen*

(1552–99), as a winged monster with the body of a dog disguised as a beautiful young woman. The little hedgehog-like critters are far less terrifying. When confronted by humans they are more likely to dig into the soil and roll into a tight ball to evade capture.

Eggs Benedict

Two conflicting tales purport to tell the origin of this simple dish, consisting of poached eggs and ham atop two English muffins and covered with hollandaise sauce. That the recipe originated in New York seems to be the only point of agreement. The Waldorf-Astoria Hotel insists that a hungover customer, Samuel Benedict, sauntered in one day and requested a cure for his throbbing temples. At the famous Delmonico's restaurant, so the rival story goes, two regulars, a Mr and Mrs LeGrand Benedict, were disappointed with the contents of the menu. They asked the chef to whip up something new and were presented with their own eponymous meal.

Einstein

Bookish schoolchildren and smartalecs the world over are referred to as 'regular Einsteins', making the name of the great nuclear physicist not only a byword for brilliance but nerdishness too (Einstein would be amused; he was famously bad at mathematics at school). German-born Albert Einstein (1879–1955) has also been justifiably honoured by the scientific community. The first eponymous application of his name accompanied a solar eclipse in 1919. His general theory of relativity, published three years earlier, had predicted that light waves were influenced by gravity. The eclipse proved him right and the phenomenon became known as the **Einstein**

shift. The **einstein** is a unit of light used in photochemistry and a synthetic chemical element discovered in the debris of a hydrogen bomb explosion in 1952 was named **einsteinium** (Es), atomic number 99. The same year Einstein was offered – and turned down – the presidency of Israel, preferring to live out his final years in the relative seclusion of Princeton University. Einstein's concerns about advances in German nuclear research led directly to the development of the atomic bomb, although he played no part in its construction.

Electra complex

Psychological condition describing a daughter's subconscious attraction to her father and corresponding hatred for her mother. In Greek mythology, Electra was the daughter of Agamemnon, the king of Mycenae. In the tragedies by Sophocles (*c.* 418–410 BC) and Euripides (*c.* 413 BC), Electra seeks to avenge the death of Agamemnon by persuading her brother to murder their mother.

Éminence grise

One who exerts power without formal appointment or acclamation. The Capuchin monk and statesman, Père Joseph, originally François-Joseph Le Clerc du Tremblay (1577–1638), wielded great influence on French foreign policy under the patronage of Louis XIII's chief minister, Cardinal Richelieu. The obsessive desire of the former noble to reclaim the Holy Land complemented Richelieu's plans to restore French influence in Europe by subjugating the continent's Protestant population and re-establishing the primacy of Catholicism. At the side of his patron, known as *l'éminence rouge* – 'the red eminence', Joseph came to be perceived as a shadowy character and earned the tag *l'éminence grise* or 'the grey eminence'.

Epicurean

Person devoted to the refined enjoyment of the best things in life. The Greek philosopher Epicurus (341–271 BC) taught that pleasure equated with wisdom and was therefore the highest virtue. His hedonistic ideas inspired ridicule but also laid the grounds for serious scientific study. Epicurus was an early proponent of chaos theory, believing that life was the result of a chance combination of atoms.

Erotic

Pertaining to sexual desire. Eros, the winged god of love, was usually depicted as a child meddling in the affairs of the human heart, inciting desire with his arrows. He was not immune to arousal himself, most notably falling in love with Psyche (*see* **Cupid** and **psyche**).

Fabergé egg

Jewel-encrusted baubles originally made for the Russian imperial family and given as gifts to foreign aristocrats. Peter Carl Fabergé, real name Karl Gustavovich Fabergé (1846–1920), learnt his craft at the feet of his father and inherited the St Petersburg jewellers in 1870. His decision to branch out from jewellery to make purely decorative works distinguished him from his contemporaries and his creations were much admired throughout Europe. The first of the famous Easter eggs was fashioned for the tsaritsa in 1884 and commissioned by Emperor Alexander III. Fabergé was forced to flee Russia in the wake of the 1917 revolution and died in exile in Lausanne three years later.

Fabian

Socialist society affiliated to the Labour party which advocates gradual political change, especially the intervention of the state to increase social welfare. Established in 1884, its founding members included George Bernard Shaw and Sidney and Beatrice Webb. The Fabians took their name from Quintus Fabius Maximus Cunctator (d.203 BC), a Roman general whose patient and elusive tactics in avoiding pitched battle secured his ultimate victory over Hannibal's stronger forces. The surname Cunctator translates as 'delayer'.

Fagin

Euphemism for a thief or a person who instructs children in the art of theft, after the leader of the band of youthful pickpockets in *Oliver Twist* (1838) by Charles Dickens (*see* **Dickensian**). Like Shylock (*see* **Shylock**) in Shakespeare's *Merchant of Venice*, the cowardly Fagin is a stereotypical Jewish character in English fiction. He had a real-life counterpart in Ikey Solomons, convicted for receiving stolen goods in 1831 and incarcerated at Newgate Gaol.

Fahrenheit

Temperature scale. When German physicist Gabriel Daniel Fahrenheit (1686–1736) set out to construct a reliable thermometer, there were more than thirty different temperature scales in use, none of which corresponded with any other. In 1714 Fahrenheit replaced alcohol with mercury to produce the most accurate thermometer to date. He set the freezing point of water at 32°F and boiling point at 212°F. The precision of the instrument led to the adoption of the Fahrenheit scale in most English-speaking countries. Latterly it has been superseded by the centigrade scale, measured in degrees Celcius (*see* **Celsius**), but Fahreheit's calibrations are still in use, most notably in the US. Fahrenheit spent most of his working life in Holland and died at The Hague.

Fallopian tubes

Tubes leading from the ovaries to the uterus, discovered by the celebrated anatomist of renaissance Italy, Gabrielle Falloppio (1523–62). His masterwork, *Observationes anatomicae* (1561), was a milestone in medical texts describing for the first time the workings of many parts of the human body, such as the inner ear. Falloppio is also regarded as the first champion of the condom (*see* **condom**), advocating (*c.* 1550) the use of sheep's intestines knotted at one end to prevent the onset of syphilis (*see* **syphilis**).

Fauna

Animals. In classical legend, Fauna coupled with Hercules and bore a son, Latinus, the progenitor of the Roman people. When Hercules departed, she married her brother, Faunus, a rural deity who protected shepherds and their flocks. Fauna is portrayed as a beautiful young woman.

Fedora

Soft felt hat with a low crown and broad brim, apparently named after the title character of a popular nineteenth-century stage play. *Fédora*, by French playwright Victorien Sardou, told the tragic tale of a Russian princess, Fédora Romanoff. The drama was a big hit when it transferred to the US stage the next year.

Fender

Trademark name for a range of electric guitars developed by Californian Leo Fender (1909–91). The solid-bodied instruments had their origin in the amplifiers which manufacturers were producing for conventional acoustic guitars. Fender's Telecaster, originally called the Broadcaster, was introduced in 1948 and remains a favourite with musicians including Bruce Springsteen. Its successor, the 1953 Stratocaster, was popularized by performers as diverse as Buddy Holly, Eric Clapton and Jimi

Hendrix. Convinced he had not long to live, Fender sold his company to CBS in 1965. He made a complete recovery and continued to design new instruments, which were less successful than their predecessors.

Fermium (Fm)

Chemical element, symbol Fm, atomic number 100. Italian scientist Enrico Fermi (1901–54) won the Nobel Prize for physics in 1938 but fearing Mussolini's rule fled with his family to the US. In the basement squash court at the University of Chicago he changed the course of history: building the first nuclear reactor and producing for the first time a controlled flow of energy from a source other than the sun. Fermi's work led directly to the development of the atomic bomb and the nuclear power industry. In 1952, a new chemical element artifically produced by bombarding plutonium with neutrons was dubbed fermium in his honour. The term **fermi** was also adopted as a unit of length for nuclear distances. He was also the inaugural recipient of the awards for work in nuclear physics bestowed by the US Atomic Energy Commission that now bear his name.

Ferris wheel

The evergreen fairground attraction made its debut at the 1892 Columbian World's Exposition in Chicago as America's answer to the Eiffel Tower that had been such a sensation at the Paris exposition three years earlier. The original ferris wheel was designed and constructed by Illinois engineer George Washington Gale Ferris (1859–96) who was more used to constructing bridges and railroads. It measured 250 feet in diameter and had thirty-six carriages each capable of carrying up to sixty people: in all the big wheel could hold as many as 2,000 passengers at one time.

Filbert

Variety of hazel nut, *Corylus maxima*, once plentiful throughout Britain but largely replaced by the Kentish cob, developed in the nineteenth century. The nut is reputedly named after the French saint and founder of monasteries, Philibert (*c.* AD 608 to *c.* 685), whose feast day, 20 August, falls as the hazel nuts are collected. He was celebrated in Britain following the Norman conquests. Alternatively, the furry husk may account for the early spelling of the name, *filberd* or full beard.

Flora

Plants and flowers. The personification of plant life, from the Roman goddess of fertility and flowers of the same name. Ovid records that Flora was originally a nymphy called Chloris, who was swept off her feet by the god of wind, Zephyr. As a token of his affection, she was deified and granted power over everything that blossoms.

Foley artist

Motion picture sound-effects technician who dubs in additional audio in post-production, such as footsteps or punches. Such specialists were named in honour of Jack Foley, the United Artists soundman who devised many of the techniques in the 1930s. Among his feats, Foley replicated the sound of Niagara Falls by recording a hose splashing onto a tin advertising sign.

Forteana

Strange goings on and inexplicable phenomena were the specialist subject of New Yorker Charles Hoy Fort (1874–1932). He argued that too often scientists were influenced by their beliefs, not the evidence before them and outlined his philosophy in two published works: *The Book of the Damned* (1923) and *Wild Talents* (1932).

Fosbury flop

A style of high jumping in which the athlete leaps backwards, head first, and lands on his back. Before United States Olympian Richard Fosbury (1947–) won the gold medal at the 1968 games in Mexico City competitors would attempt to straddle the bar.

Foucault pendulum

Large mass, originally a heavy iron ball, suspended from a long wire that was used to prove that the earth rotated on its axis. French physicist Jean-Bernard-Léon Foucault (1819–68) constructed such a device in 1851 and carried out a celebrated public demonstration at the Panthéon in Paris to prove his theory. He also built the first gyroscope to further illustrate his point. At the same time Foucault began research to determine the speed of light. His calculations announced in 1862 proved astonishingly accurate for the day, within one per cent of the true figure.

Foxtrot

Ballroom dance alternating between both slow and quick steps popularized in the United States before the First World War. It has been suggested that the dance is named after Henry Fox, a Ziegfeld Follies comic. Alternatively, the name may be derived from the fashion for calling dance steps after animals. Other examples from the time include the turkey trot and the horse trot.

Frangipani

The Marquis Muzio Frangipani was a sixteenth-century Roman noble, whose main claim to fame was the invention of a perfume with which to scent gloves. Italian citizens had a wry dig at the marquis by appropriating his name for the pungent white or pink tubular flowers, *Plumeria rubra*, discovered in the New World. The name translates literally as 'break bread' and a variation, **frangipane**, became the name of a pastry filled with almond-flavoured cream.

Freesia

Genus of herbaceous plants of the iris family grown for their fragrant pink, white or yellow tubular flowers. The plant of southern African origin takes its name from German physician Friedrich Heinrich Theodior Freese (d. 1876).

Freudian slip

Slip of the tongue that inadvertently reveals a person's true feelings. The science of psychoanalysis, founded by Austrian Sigmund Freud (1856–1939), sets out to explain man's neuroses by understanding the workings of the subconscious. Freud's correlation between dreams and repressed sexual desires has also had a major impact on twentieth-century art. When the Nazis invaded, the Jewish doctor was obliged to leave Vienna and his post as professor of neuropathology at the city's university. He lived out his remaining year in London.

Friday

Sixth day of the week which honours the Norse goddess of love and fertility, Freya or Frigg. She equates with her Roman counterpart Venus (who gives her name to the French word for Friday, *vendredi*). Freya is the wife of the god of wisdom, Odin, whose Germanic derivation is invoked every Wednesday (*see* **Wednesday**).

Fuchsia

Genus of subtropical trees and shrubs that bear attractive purple flowers. German botanist and physician Leonhard Fuchs (1501–66) taught medicine at the University of Tübingen; his main sphere of interest being the medicinal properties of plant life. In 1542 he published an encyclopaedic volume on natural history, the first such compendium to be decorated with detailed illustrations of each distinctive species.

Galenic medicines

Over-the-counter medicines; drugs sanctioned by health authorities. Greek physician and anatomist Galen (AD 129–*c*. 199) was the most renowned authority on drugs and remedies of his age; his work was regarded as the last word on medicine for the next 1,000 years. He published anatomical works and carried out many dissections, proving, for instance, that arteries carried blood and not air. Galen travelled extensively and was called to Rome to become the chief physician to Emperor Marcus Aurelius and his successors.

Gallup poll

Opinion survey that strategically targets a cross section of the population. In 1932 journalism lecturer George Horace Gallup (1901–84) was engaged by an advertising agency to determine the popularity of its products. Within four years he had established his company, the Institute of Public Polling, in both Britain and the US. The accuracy of his election forecasts engendered public confidence in his methods. Yet Gallup and the rest of America's pollsters still forecast the defeat of President Harry S. Truman in the 1948 presidential race. Truman won.

Galvanize

To stir into action by shock or excitement; to coat with metal, usually to protect against rust. Luigi Galvani (1737–98), a professor of anatomy at Bologna University, discovered that frogs' legs would twitch when they came into contact with metal during a thunderstorm and, later, when touched by two different metals. He mistakenly concluded that the muscles and nerves produced 'animal electricity'. Alessandro Volta, who would later invent the battery, showed that dissimilar metals were responsible for generating the electric charge. An early Italian patriot, Galvani lost his university post in 1796 when he refused to swear allegiance to Napoleon's rule and died, grief stricken, the following year. The **galvanometer**, a device capable of measuring small electric currents and named in Galvani's honour, was invented in 1820 by André Ampère (*see* **ampere**).

Gamp

Drunken and disreputable woman so called after Sarah Gamp, the midwife who bore these traits in Charles Dickens' *Martin Chuzzlewit* (1843). The name is also given to a large unwieldy umbrella similar to the type carried by the character.

Gardenia

Evergreen shrub native to subtropical Africa and Asia, which bears fragrant white and yellow flowers. Scottish naturalist Doctor Alexander Garden (1730–91) was a friend of the Swedish Botanist, Carolus Linnaeus, and an inveterate collector of botanical and mineralogical specimens. He emigrated to South Carolina in 1754 and remained loyal to the Crown throughout the Revolutionary War. Bitterly disappointed by its outcome, he returned to England at the conclusion of the conflict. His son, however, went back to the US and fought in the Continental Army.

Gargantuan

Gigantic. In Celtic myth, Gargantua was a giant with a large appetite; he was also the subject, with his son, of Rabelais' five-volume satire *Pantagruel* and *Gargantua* (written between 1532 and 1564). Rabelais ran into trouble with religious leaders who regarded his work as blasphemous.

Garibaldi

Italian nationalist leader Guiseppe Garibaldi (1807–82) had a weak spot for pastries baked with a layer of currants, hence a type of sweet biscuit commercially produced from the late nineteenth century. He also gave his name to a bright red long-sleeved blouse for women and children, which evoked the garb worn by the 'Redshirts', Garibaldi's volunteer army. This arose by accident while the exiled Garibaldi was raising his first Italian legion in Uruguay. War with Argentina had restricted trade and the Uruguayan government gave the Italian soldiers a consignment of red shirts no longer destined for export. They carried them back to Italy in 1848 and finally liberated Italy from French and Austrian occupation in 1861.

Gatling gun

The most reliable of the early machine guns. Moral and ethical questions are often secondary concerns in the arms trade, but US gunsmith Richard Jordan Gatling (1818-1903) was positively traitorous. Gatling, a southerner, moved from North Carolina to Indiana in 1844 to capitalize on the north's superior technological capabilities and the greater finances available to fund his inventions. He began work on the new weapon as the Civil War began and was awarded a patent the following year in 1862; he even wrote to Abraham Lincoln suggesting the gun be used 'as a means in crushing this rebellion'. All the while he was an active member of a secret group of Confederate activists. Ironically, it was only after the war ended that Gatling began to fill his order books, with sales to the US, British, Russian, Turks and Spanish. The Gatling gun was fired by turning a hand crank that would turn a revolving cylinder containing six-gun barrels, firing up to 400 bullets in one minute.

Gauss

Unit measuring the density of magnetic flux, named after the remarkable German mathematician and astronomer, Karl Friedrich Gauss (1777–1855). While still a boy, Gauss established many principles of modern algebra and geometry, some of which were not recognized until after his death. He independently calculated the distance between the planets and the sun, known as Bode's Law (*see* **Bode's law**), before his seventeenth birthday and published his influential theory of numbers *Disquisitiones arithmeticae* in 1801. He later conducted research into electricity and magnetism, constructing an electromagnetic telegraph system in 1831 with fellow scientist Wilhelm Weber. The term **degauss** entered common usage early in World War II to describe a process by which a magnetic field is removed from a ship. A cable containing an electric current is passed over the ship, rendering it non-magnetic and protecting the vessel from magnetic mines.

Geiger counter

Apparatus used to measure radiation in the air. German scientist Hans Wilhelm Geiger (1882–1945) built the first such device at Manchester University in 1908 with the British physicist Ernest Rutherford. The radioactive particles pass into a gas-filled tube containing an electrode; as the particles become electrically charged they conduct pulses of current. As Professor of Physics at Kiel University, Geiger and a colleague, W. Müller, continued to improve the counter by increasing its sensitivity. The pair produced the prototype of the modern instrument in 1928, which is more correctly known as the Geiger-Müller counter.

Georgette

Thin crêpe material, usually made of silk and used in dressmaking. It is said to have been designed by Georgette de la Plante, a famous milliner in nineteenth-century Paris and was widely used in Britain by the early twentieth century.

Geronimo!

Tall tales abound but there is no definitive explanation why US paratroopers adopted as their battle cry the name of the great Apache Indian leader. One version tells how a raw recruit of the 82nd Airborne Division was inspired by the screening of a Hollywood film about the famous chief and uttered the name on his first jump the following day. Another version suggests that soliders at Fort Sill in Oklahoma were told the story of Geronimo's attempts to evade capture in the nearby hills by making a breathtaking jump from a cliff face onto horseback. The story stretches credibility somewhat: Fort Sills was an artillery and guided-missile school not a paratroop-training camp. The surrender of Geronimo (1829–1908), whose name means 'one who yawns', in Mexico in 1886 brought the Indian Wars to a close. He was removed to Florida and later Oklahoma, the US Government having retracted its promise to let Geronimo return to his native Arizona.

Gerrymander

To redistribute electoral boundaries in order to favour a particular political party. Massachusetts Governor Elbridge Gerry (1744–1814) redrew the state's political map in 1812. Political cartoonist Gilbert Stuart suggested the new boundaries of one particular district resembled a salamander, to which the editor of the *Boston Sentinel*, Benjamin Russell, replied, 'No, a gerrymander.' Gerry later became Vice President in the administration of James Madison.

Gibson guitar

Trademark name for a range of electric guitars produced by the company founded by Orville H. Gibson in 1903 and used by musicians including BB King and Elvis Presley. Yet the firm was initially reticent about the **Les Paul Gibson**, the instrument that was to become its biggest seller and the industry standard. Musician Les Paul (1915–2009) was disappointed by the guitars he was being asked to play in the 1940s and set about designing a solid-bodied model. Gibson began production but insisted that the instrument should not carry its name. As sales grew, the company reversed its policy.

Gideon Bible

Chances are if you are staying in a hotel there will be a Gideon Bible in the bottom drawer of the bedside table, bearing the distinctive symbol of a pitcher and flame. Gideon was the biblical liberator of the Israelites whose story is told in the Book of Judges. With an army of 300 men he overthrew the Midianites, a tribe who worshipped a false god. It was in honour of this battle that three men in Wisconsin established the international Christian society that distributes Bibles to hotels, hospitals and prisons. Gideon kept busy siring seventy-one sons but the Israelites began bickering again upon his death.

Gladstone bag

Leather suitcase with a hinged opening. Liverpudlian William Ewart Gladstone (1809–98) was the Grand Old Man of British politics, four times Prime Minister before leaving office half blind and half deaf in 1895, aged eighty-five. In all, he spent sixty-three years at Westminster battling against his nemesis Benjamin Disraeli with his oratorical skills. 'Oh, William dear,' remarked Mrs Gladstone, 'if you weren't such a great man what a bore you would be.' When as Chancellor of the Exchequer he lowered the duty on French wine, the cheapest alcohol became known as **Gladstone sherry** or **Gladstone brandy** accordingly. In his spare time Gladstone was known to trawl the dimly lit streets of London's West End attempting to redeem prostitutes, much to the horror of his allies and after which the eminent Victorian statesman would invariably flagellate himself.

Golliwog

The black-faced toy, described as 'a horrid sight', first appeared in a children's book, *The Adventures of two Dutch Girls and a 'Golliwogg'* (1895), by English author Bertha Upton (1849–1912). Both the character and its distinctive shaggy appearance were invented by the book's illustrator, the author's US-born daughter Florence K. Upton (1873–1922). Other adventures followed, precipitating a golliwog craze at the turn of the century but Upton neglected to copyright her creation, foregoing the substantial royalties that would have accrued. The decline in the popularity of the toy, now seen as essentially a negative racial stereotype, coincided with the rise of the US civil-rights movement. In Britain the golliwog was officially 'retired' from appearing on jars of preserves made by the Manchester firm of James Robertson & Sons in 2002.

Gordian knot

To cut the Gordian knot is to solve a problem by decisive action. Gordias, the mythical founder of the Phrygian capital, tied his chariot to the wall of the citadel and declared that the complicated knot could only be undone by the conqueror of the empire of Asia. Alexander the Great heard the story on entering the city of Gordium in 333 BC and immediately cut the knot with his sword. Gordium was razed by the Cimmerians (who gave their name to the Crimea) in the seventh century BC. A peasant, Gordias, and the Phrygian mother of the gods, Cybele, were the parents of Midas (*see* **Midas touch**).

Gordon Bennett

Mild expression of displeasure that, like 'gosh', neatly avoids invoking the name of the deity. Scottish-born US journalist James Gordon Bennett (1795–1892) was the pre-eminent American newspaperman of the nineteenth century. He founded the *New York Herald* in 1835 and pioneered many modern newsgathering techniques, establishing foreign bureaux and introducing financial reporting. His son and successor of the same name (1841–1918) recognized the commercial potential of sponsorship and attached his name to motor and air races. Without his nose for news we would certainly never have heard the famous expression, 'Doctor Livingstone, I presume?' In 1869, Bennett Jnr sent a two-word cable to his reporter Henry Morton Stanley: 'Find Livingstone.' He did. The famous meeting took place at Lake Tanganyika in 1871.

Gordon setter

Hunting dog, originally called 'black and tan setters', introduced in 1820 by Charles Gordon-Lennox, the 5th Duke of Richmond

and Gordon (1791–1860) at Gordon Castle in Morayshire. Richmond followed his father into the military, where he served as an aide-de-camp to Wellington in Portugal. Ironically, on his elevation to the Tory benches of the House of Lords he became a staunch political foe of Wellington and vigorously opposed the Catholic Emancipation Bill. In 1830 Richmond was called upon to quell 200 rioting farm labourers in Sussex; with the aid of fifty tenant farmers and, by employing his characteristic wit, he sent the mob away in good spirits.

Gore-Tex

Trademark name for a light, breathable fabric containing billions of microscopic pores per square inch and made from strands of the polymer, Teflon. It was devised in the 1960s by former Du Pont research chemist Wilbert L. Gore and his chemist son Robert Gore in the basement of their family home. Gore-Tex clothing was initially plagued with troubles, absorbing sweat and being far too bulky. The membrane was redesigned, made impervious to body oils and laminated onto soft fabrics. Sales soared. The porous material is also used to make artificial body parts.

Gorgon

Denoting ugliness. The three Gorgons of Greek mythology, Medusa, Stheno and Euryale were so frightening that their gaze was enough to turn men into stone. Each possessed snakes on their heads instead of hair, scaly necks and sharp protruding teeth. In Homer's version of the story a single Gorgon, previously a beautiful girl who was punished for her presumptuousness by the jealous Athena, roamed the underworld.

Granny Smith

Variety of green cooking apple first cultivated by Australian Anne Smith in the Sydney suburb of Ryde. Mrs Smith discovered a sapling growing where she had left the remains of some apples; it is believed the new variety grew from the seed of a French crab apple. The trees were propagated and the fruit first exported to Britain in the 1830s. A public park in Ryde is dedicated to the memory of 'Granny' Smith.

Greengage plum

Type of fruit. In the early eighteenth century, a Suffolk landowner Sir William Gage (1777–1864) imported to England from France a new variety of plum tree. He planted the first seedling in the garden of his property near Bury St Edmunds *c.*1725 and noted that the ripened fruit had a greenish tinge. In France the greengage had long been known as the *reinclaude*, after Claude of Brittany, the first wife of the extravagant monarch Francis I.

Gregorian calendar

The reform of the calendar introduced by Julius Caesar in 46 BC represented a marked improvement in the measurement of the planet's annual passage, but still there was one substantial flaw. The Julian year was eleven minutes longer than the solar year and by the late sixteenth century the calendar was again seriously out of kilter. Pope Gregory XIII employed the Neapolitan astronomer Luigi Lilio Ghiraldi and German Jesuit Christopher Clavius to correct the anomaly and lopped off ten whole days from the month of October in 1582. Over the next five years the Gregorian calendar was adopted by most Catholic countries. Britain and her dominions followed suit in 1752, when people went to bed on 2 September and woke up the next morning on 14 September. Other countries, particularly in the East, were reluctant to alter religious calendars; Russia was just plain sluggish, finally introducing the changes in 1918.

Gregorian chant

Ritual songs of devotion performed without musical accompaniment, introduced during the papacy of Gregory I, also known as Gregory the Great (c. 540 to c. 604). The first monk to become pope, Gregory's reform of the Liturgy and emphasis on missionary work were to have a widespread influence on the medieval church. A skillful administrator, he quelled the invading Lombards, relieved distress caused by plague, famine and flood and arranged Augustine's mission to convert the Anglo-Saxons. He also insisted on the humility of church officials. To this day the Pope still bears Gregory's preferred title, 'servant of the servants of God'.

Guillotine

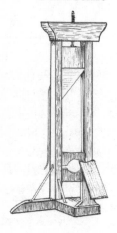

Device for beheading people. The French Revolution overthrew not only the previous way of life, but the manner of death as well. Until 1792, decapitation was a privilege of the aristocracy. Now Frenchmen of all stations could die in the same fashion and Madame La Guillotine was busily employed in performing her patriotic duty. Her first victim was a humble highwayman but Louis XVI and

Marie Antoinette soon followed, as did leaders of the Revolution including Robespierre. The device was the invention of a surgeon, Antoine Louis (1723–92), and was briefly known as the Louisette (similar designs had been in use since the fourteenth century). However, the instrument came to be named after its champion, Joseph Ignace Guillotin (1734–1814), a physician who advocated its use as a humanitarian method of execution. The word entered the English language the year following its introduction and came to mean terrible slaughter and a handy item of office equipment used for cutting paper. Since the 1890s, it has also been applied to the premature cessation of parliamentary debates.

Guppy

Small freshwater fish, *Lebistes reticulatus* and *Poecilia reticulata*, native to the West Indies. A clergyman stationed in Trinidad, Robert John Lechmore Guppy (1836–1916), forwarded the first specimens to the British Museum in 1866. The colourful species are a familiar feature of home aquariums.

Guy

US slang for a man; effigy of the soldier Guy Fawkes (1570–1606) burned on bonfire night every 5 November. Fawkes was the ballistics expert called in to aid the Gunpowder Plot, the Catholic conspiracy to blow up James I at the opening of the Houses of Parliament on 5 November 1605. The plot was exposed when one of the conspirators told a relative, who subsequently informed the authorities. When the cellars of the House of Lords were searched, they found both Fawkes and the gunpowder. He was tortured into revealing the names of his seven co-conspirators. His injuries were so severe that when he was hanged in January of the following year, Fawkes needed assistance to mount the gallows. The cellars are still ceremonially searched every year before the state opening of Parliament by the Queen. The report of the warden who discovered the gunpowder is often on public display at Westminster.

Halley's comet

Bright celestial body. In 1703 the Professor of Geometry at Oxford University, Edmund (or Edmond) Halley (1656–1742), applied Newton's (*see* **newton**) theory of gravitation to the Great Comet, which had passed over the planet twenty years previously. He suggested that this and similar comets observed in 1456, 1531 and 1607 were one and the same and calculated that it would return in 1758. His hypothesis proved correct and Halley was hailed posthumously. Halley began his scientific career charting the stars of the southern hemisphere at St Helena, later to become the island prison of Napoleon Bonaparte. He was appointed Astronomer Royal at Greenwich in 1720 and held the position until his death.

Hammond organ

Portable electric organ used in popular music, produced by the Chicago company founded by Laurens Hammond. The first electronic organ was designed by two French inventors in 1930 and used radio lamps and amplifiers to reproduce the sounds of a pipe organ. However, electricity had been used to control the pipes of conventional organs since 1895. The original unit invented by Hammond in 1935 used a rotating 'tone wheel' to generate the requisite frequencies. The public appreciated its portability and the Hammond organ found a ready market.

Hansard

Official record of parliamentary proceedings. Until the nineteenth century, the reporting of debates was unlawful. When the House relaxed its restrictions, the journalist William Cobbett engaged the services of printer Luke Hansard (1752–1828) to publish his reports. The printer's son, Thomas Curson Hansard (1776–1833), took over the series in 1812. It was a risky enterprise; the publication of debates was still unofficial and Hansard attracted libel writs from individuals criticized under parliamentary privilege. He was even sent to prison for printing Cobbett's denunciation of military flogging. Hansard's firm, later assisted by a Government grant, was subsequently replaced by a succession of contractors and Parliament's own staff of reporters, introduced in 1908.

Hansom cab

Two-wheeled horse-drawn carriage. The original hansom cab, designed in 1834 by a Birmingham civil architect J. Aloysius Hanson (1803–82), bore little resemblance to the famous vehicle which was to become the predecessor of the London taxi. The large, box-like carriage had two enormous wheels seven feet in diameter and passengers were forced to sit next to the driver. The more familiar light-weight carriage, essentially a souped-up gig, was built two years later and the patent sold to the Hansom Cab Company by its designer, John Chapman. The cabman sat, exposed to the elements, behind the passengers and controlled the horse with a pair of long reins. Throughout the latter half of the

nineteenth century, passengers, policemen and parliamentarians fought a running battle to force the cabmen to reduce their fares. Prosecutions did much to raise the standing of policemen in the eyes of the public and established the reputation of the helpful bobby (*see* **bobby**).

Hays Office

Common name for the bureau established by the Motion Picture Producers and Distributors of America to enforce a strict moral censorship code. Its first director was Will H. Hays (1879-1954), a dour former Republican Party chairman and postmaster-general in the administration of Warren G. Harding. In the 1920s Hollywood had feared that the growing risqué content of its films, not to mention the debauched lifestyle of its contract players, would lead inevitably to heavy-handed legislation. The movie moguls headed the politicians off at the pass and drafted their own Production Code, formally introduced in 1934, which banned 'excessive and lustful kissing, lustful embracing, suggestive postures and gestures' etc. The ban on blatant sexuality and graphic violence arguably broadened the skill of filmmakers who had to devise new techniques to impart their messages. The code was abolished in 1968.

Heath Robinson contraption

Improbable machines and mechanical inventions named after the complex contraptions drawn for *Punch* by cartoonist William Heath Robinson (1872–1944). A real-life contraption called Heath Robinson helped win World War II. The early prototype computer was a teletype machine which was capable of reading 2,000 characters per minute. It was put into service in 1943 to help decode enemy messages. Unfortunately it had a nasty habit of chewing up the paper it was meant to be reading. In American parlance, crackpot machines are known as Rube Goldberg inventions.

Herculean

A herculean task is one performed with great effort. When Hercules is induced by a jealous Juno (*see* **junoesque**) into killing his wife and children, Apollo enslaves him to the Mycenaean king, the hero's cousin Eurystheus, for twelve years. He is forced to carry out twelve tasks which require his physical strength, including cleaning out the Augean stables (*see* **Augean stables**). In return for the successful completion of his labours, Hercules is granted immortality. The story equates with the tale of the Greek hero, Heracles.

Hermaphrodite

A creature or plant that possesses both male and female characteristics or reproductive organs. In spite of the persistent advances of the nymph Salmacis, the god Hermaphroditus, son of Hermes and Aphrodite, would have nothing to do with her. She asked the other gods for help and when Hermaphroditus dived into a lake, he was merged with Salmacis into a single entity. Thereafter, according to legend, all males who swam in the lake in Caria lost their masculinity.

Hertz

Unit of frequency, identified by the symbol 'Hz'. German physicist Heinrich Rudolph Hertz (1857–94) confirmed Maxwell's theory of the existence of electromagnetic radiation, specifically radio waves, when he was able to produce a spark in a gap between two conducting wires. His experiment paved the way for the modern radio communications industry. Hertz also discovered the speed of radio waves and the speed of light are one and the same.

Hippocratic oath

The 2,000-year-old oath of allegiance sworn by medical practitioners to uphold ethical practice. Hippocrates (c. 460 to c. 377) is regarded as the Father of Medicine and the greatest physician of ancient Greece. The medical works known as the Hippocratic Collection outline his philosophy to 'prescribe regimen for the good of my patients according to my ability and my judgement and never do harm to anyone'. Many of the documents, including the famous oath, are believed to be the work of Hippocrates' followers, who studied at the medical school he established on Cos, the island of his birth.

Hobson's choice

No alternative. The phrase supposedly originates with the noted Cambridge stable-keeper Thomas Hobson (1544?–1631) who, it is said, would only hire out his horses in strict rotation. One contemporary account recorded that 'every customer was alike well served according to his chance, and every horse ridden with the same justice'. However, doubt has been cast on this accepted etymology. The term 'Hodgson's choice' – 'such privilegese as they will geve us, or else goe without' – has been recorded as early as 1617.

Hodgkin's disease

Disease that causes the body's lymphatic glands to enlarge and is responsible for a high incidence of anaemia. The complaint was first described by a pathologist at Guy's Hospital in London, Thomas Hodgkin (1798–1866). Radiotherapy and chemotherapy are used to combat the disease, the cause of which is unknown.

Hooligan

Rowdy person; violent thug. For many years it was thought that the term originated with a stereotypical London Irish family, the Houlihans or Hooligans, celebrated in the English music hall, or the salacious exploits of Patrick Hooligan, a violent criminal who stalked Victorian London. The chronicle of Hooligan's career, published in 1899, told how he 'walked among his fellow men, robbing them and occasionally bashing them'. He was sentenced to life imprisonment for assaulting a police officer (Hooligan 'put his lights out, and threw the body into a dust-cart'; the criminal died in hospital not long after beginning his incarceration). But disgraceful behaviour was being ascribed to characters of the same name or similar spelling at least seventy-five years earlier. The farce, *More Blunders than One* (1824), contains a drunken Irish valet called Larry Hoolagan.

Hoover

To vacuum; trademark name for a vacuum cleaner. In 1907 a new device called the 'electric suction sweeper' came to the attention of an Ohio leather-goods manufacturer, William Henry Hoover (1849–1942). The appliance, invented by a nightwatchman called J. Murray Spangler, was the prototype of the household vacuum cleaner. The smooth-talking Hoover immediately saw its potential and Spangler agreed to sell him the rights. The following year the Hoover Suction Company launched the Model 'O' domestic cleaner, priced at a hefty $70. In fact, an Englishman, Hubert Cecil Booth, had invented virtually the same machine way back in 1901. The difference was the British saw only the potential for industrial use. Booth's Vacuum Cleaning Company hawked its bulky machines from office to office, not giving the domestic market a moment's thought.

Hotspur

An impetuous person; one who displays the restless energy of the fourteenth-century noble Sir Henry Percy (1364–1403). Percy was 'intolerant of the shadow of a slight' and earned the nickname Hatspore or Hotspur for his long and valiant skirmishes with Scottish invaders. His reckless revolt against Henry IV, merely served to justify the sobriquet. In 1386 he was sent to Calais to preempt a French attack. Tired of waiting, the impetuous Percy mounted his own raids instead. He was killed in the Battle of Shrewsbury and, it is said, the king shed a tear for his old friend, the son of the 1st Earl of Northumberland. Percy's head was removed to York and mounted on a gate as a warning to others. The character of Harry Hotspur appears in William Shakespeare's historical plays *Richard II* and *Henry IV Part I*.

Houdini

Person able to extricate himself from a tight spot; escapologist. Hungarian-born US magician Harry Houdini, real name Erik Weisz (1874–1926), remains the world's best-known conjurer. His most famous feats involved trying to escape from weighted boxes immersed in water, often with his hands bound or cuffed. Houdini bragged that he could always take a punch unawares. He couldn't. The performer died from perionitis after a student put him to the test. Houdini took his stage name from a renowned French illusionist Jean Eugène Robert Houdin (1805–71).

Hubble Space Telescope

Astronomical reflecting telescope launched into orbit round the earth in 1990. It is no exaggeration to say that the work of US astronomer Edwin Powell Hubble (1889–1953) extended the bounds of the known universe. From the Mount Wilson Observatory in Pasadena, he discovered that the cloudy nebulae in outer space were in fact other galaxies. In 1929, **Hubble's constant** stated that the universe was expanding – galaxies were moving away from one another, at a rate of speed that increased with distance. Hubble was frustrated by the limitations of early twentieth-century telescopes and probably would have marvelled at the £2.5 billion spacecraft that takes his name. It is free from atmospheric interferences and uses computers to enhance the resolution of the objects in view.

Hygiene

Health and cleanliness, from Hygieia, the Greek goddess of health. She is identified by a symbol depicting a serpent supping from a bowl in her hand. Hygieia was one of the five daughters of Asclepius, the god of medicine and healing.

Jack Russell terrier

Short-legged terriers with smooth black and white or tan coats. Enter the harness room at the Royal residence at Sandringham and you will discover a painting of the mother of the Jack Russell breed. Parson John Russell (1795–1883) struck up a life-long friendship with the Prince of Wales, later Edward VII, while adjudicating at a dog show in Plymouth. The parson was a familiar face at canine competitions well into old age, a founder member of the Kennel Club and a passionate hunter in his native Derbyshire (which makes one wonder how much time he had left to devote to the ministrations of his flock). Above all, he swore to produce the ideal terrier that would root out foxes from their holes, giving the hounds and the hunt followers a good chase. As a student, lazily punting up the Cherwell, near Oxford, he spied the perfect candidate walking alongside her master, a milkman. Russell succeeded in persuading the owner to sell him the bitch, called Trump, on the spot. The breed became widely admired and on Russell's death the future monarch bought the portrait of Trump, which he removed to Sandringham.

Jacquard loom

Frenchman Joseph Marie Jacquard (1752–1834) invented a drawloom in 1801 that simplified and hastened textile production. Attached to the loom was a rotating series of punch cards that controlled the weaving of the pattern. The punch cards inspired the designers of the first programmable computers more than a century later; the machine itself became the prototype for automated machinery in modern textile mills. Like the sewing machine before it (*see* **Singer sewing machine**), the jacquard loom raised fears among manual workers that mechanization would mean job losses. Silk weavers took to the streets, attacking Jacquard and burning his machines. By 1820 the new looms had spread worldwide and the industrial revolution had begun.

Jacuzzi

Trademark name for the whirlpool hot tub in which a constant stream of water at high pressure massages the body. Italian-born US engineer Candido Jacuzzi (1903–86), whose company

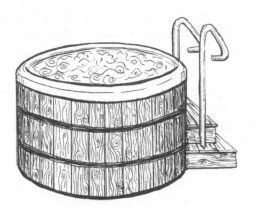

produced water pumps, devised the bath as a form of therapy for his infant son, who suffered from rheumatoid arthritis. From the 1950s it was adopted as a necessary accessory for hedonists the world over.

January

The first month honouring the ancient Roman deity Janus, the guardian of heaven. He is portrayed with two faces, one of which looks forward, the other behind, explaining the use of the word **janus** to mean any duplicitous person. According to some traditions, Janus was a Roman monarch deified upon his death. He is credited with introducing money and ancient Roman coins carry his likeness.

Jekyll and Hyde

Classic 'split personality'; wildly contradictory person. In *The Strange Case of Dr Jekyll and Mr Hyde* (1886) by Robert Louis Stevenson, the doctor attempts to rid himself of all moral impurities. Instead he creates another entity embodying all the evil characteristics he had sought to expunge. When the monster commits murder, the tortured doctor is forced to take his own life.

Jeremiah

Pessimist. An allusion to the Old Testament prophet who warned that Judah would be punished for rebelling against God. The people paid no heed and the kingdom fell to the Babylonians, led by Nebuchadnezzar, in 597 BC. In his later Lamentations, Jeremiah prays for forgiveness, comparing the destruction of Jerusalem to the fate of a fallen woman and argues that the punishment was justified. A doleful tale that invokes pity is known as a **jeremiad**.

Jeroboam

Champagne bottle, traditionally the equivalent of four normal bottles. Jeroboam was the biblical warrior of the Book of Kings who led the revolt of the tribes of greater Israel against the reign of King Solomon and his son, Rehoboam. Following an assassination attempt he escaped to Egypt, where he remained until after Solomon's death. In 931 BC Rehoboam's disastrous confirmation ceremony split the territory in two: the ten tribes to the north united behind Jeroboam; his enemy ruled over the smaller southern kingdom of Judah.

Jezebel

A brazen woman with loose morals, so called after the pagan wife of Ahab, King of Israel. The domineering Jezebel so bewitched the monarch that he built a pagan temple to worship her deity, Baal, and went along with her plot to murder one of their subjects and to take possession of his land. The widowed Jezebel died when she was thrown from a building on the orders of one of her husband's successors. Her flesh was devoured by dogs, as foretold by the prophet Elijah.

Job, patience of

The ability to endure arduous conditions with forbearance. The Old Testament story tells of a pact between God and Satan in which a blameless man is subjected to ill health, poverty and the death of his children in order to test his faith. His four friends wrongly assume that he is being punished for his sins against God; thus the term **Job's comforter** signifies a person who offers sympathy but causes distress.

John Hancock

US slang for signature, named after the largest and most legible mark that adorns the Declaration of Independence. A wealthy Massachussetts merchant, John Hancock (1737–93) fought with the Revolutionary campaigners and later served as a member of the Continental Congress, entering the history books as the first man to sign the Declaration of Independence in Philadelphia in 1776. As Governor of Massachussetts from 1780 he was initially cool towards the Federal Constitution but ratified the document nevertheless.

Joneses, keeping up with the

Aspiring to be as well off as one's neighbours, usually through the acquisition of material wealth. The term first appeared in the US early last century in a comic strip of the same name. It was in common use in Britain by the end of World War II.

Joule

Unit of heat, defined as the energy expended when a force of one newton (*see* **newton**) moves one metre. It is named after the British physicist James Prescott Joule (1818–89) who accurately calculated the amount of work needed to produce a unit of heat. Joule and his collaborator William Thomsom (*see* **kelvin**) also discovered the molecular phenomenon by which gases can cool or heat themselves, known as the **Joule-Thomson effect**.

Judas

Traitor, after Judas Iscariot who betrayed Jesus to the chief priests for a price of thirty pieces of silver. The apostle's kiss signalled Christ's identity, hence the term **Judas kiss** to mean an act of deceit. When the priests resolved to put Jesus to death, Judas suddenly realized the gravity of his action. He tried to return the money to the temple and in remorse committed suicide. In early Christian legend, the **Judas tree** or *Cercis siliquastrum* of Southern Europe was the tree on which he hanged himself.

Juggernaut

Large truck; an unstoppable force. Indians in the coastal state of Orissa would prove their devotion to the god Krishna (an incarnation of the dominant Hindu deity, Vishnu) by leaping to their death, beneath the wheels of a trolley carrying a huge idol through the streets of the city of Puri. The name comes from the Hindi *Jagganath*, a title applied to Krishna meaning 'lord of the world'. The annual procession has excited Western imagination for nearly 1,000 years. The ceremony was first described in 1321 by a visiting monk.

July

The seventh month, dedicated by Mark Antony to the Roman emperor Julius Caesar (100 BC–44 BC) whose reform of the calendar two years before his assassination remains his longest-lasting edict. Caesar overhauled the ancient Roman agricultural calendar, which began in March, and aligned the months to the passage of the sun. The insertion of leap years ensured the correction of most anomalies. Oddly enough, neither Caesar nor anyone else for that matter got around to renaming all the outdated months; we still employ many titles today which smack of irrelevance and illogicality. Granted, Quintilis or *fifth month* became July and Sextilis or *sixth month* was renamed August, after Caesar's successor, but is there any reason why the following months are still called September *month seven*, October *month eight*, November *month nine* and December *month ten*?

Jumbo

Large; a Boeing 747 jet airliner. In Victorian times an African elephant of this name became one of the most popular attractions at London Zoo. Children delighted in riding on its back and Jumbo was sold to the great American showman Phineas Taylor Barnum in 1882. It died in a railway collision three years later. The word can be traced back at least as far as the 1820s, when it was used to denote clumsiness. But the size of the elephant rather than its demeanour led to its use as a byword for anything big, including the Boeing 747, the largest aircraft in the world when it was introduced in the 1960s.

Junoesque

Beautiful. The Roman goddess Juno was the queen of heaven and the protector of women, especially in childbirth. When they made offerings to Juno (also known as Lucina) women were forbidden to wear belts or knots lest they inhibited the ability to bear children. As the mother of Mars she is also regarded as a war goddess. Her Greek equivalent is Hera. Juno is only indirectly linked to the month of **June**, which is derived from the Roman clan name Junius.

Jupiter

The largest planet with sixteen satellites, which takes more than eleven earth years to orbit round the sun. Jupiter, also known as Jove, is the most important Roman god (his Greek counterpart is Zeus) and the protector of the city of Rome itself. Emperors liked to claim a direct link; Augustus boasted that the deity sent him messages in his dreams. Astrologers believe Jupiter is the most benign planet and those born under its influence are supposed to be happy people, hence the word **jovial**. We still invoke Jupiter's name to denote surprise or displeasure in the expression '**By Jove!**'

Kafkaesque

Nightmarish disturbed state redolent of the fiction of Czech-born Austrian author, Franz Kafka (1883–1924), especially *The Trial* (1925) and *The Nightmare* (1926), both published posthumously. Kafka's work reflected his own state of despair and helplessness. In *The Trial* a man is charged with a crime he did not commit and is unable to do anything about it. Kafka came from a stable German-Jewish family but his dominant parents left him feeling isolated from other people. He moved to Berlin in the final year of his life but was forced home by deteriorating health. He died at the age of forty. Kafka left specific instructions to friends to destroy his remaining manuscripts and ensure his existing work was not republished. His wishes were ignored and he received far greater fame in death, influencing a new generation of writers and thinkers such as George Orwell and Samuel Beckett.

Kalashnikov

Common name for both the AK-47 (*automat Kalashnikov*, 1947) and AKM automatic assault rifles invented by Mikhail Timofeyevich Kalashnikov (1919–), a former Red Army tank commander. He began work on weapons development while recovering from injuries sustained in World War II. The AK-

47 was capable of firing 600 rounds per second and became the basic shoulder weapon for troops throughout the former Soviet bloc and in Soviet-sponsored guerilla actions, especially in Africa and the Middle East. The AKM was first produced in 1959; a modernized version with better sights finally replaced the AK-47 in the 1980s. Kalashnikov was much lauded at home and received the Hero of Socialist Labour award.

Kaposi's sarcoma

Malignant skin cancer resulting in purple lesions that has become increasingly common as a result of the AIDS virus. Austrian dermatologist Moritz Kohn Karposi (1837–1902) first described the symptoms, which often begin as soft reddish swellings on the hands and feet. Until recently, this was a rare complaint found primarily in Africa and among elderly men in the southern Mediterranean region. Statistics have shown that nearly half of all male homosexuals who contract AIDS develop the disease, compared to only eight per cent of all AIDS cases.

Kelvin

Thermodynamic scale allowing scientists to measure extremely low temperatures. Physicist William Thompson (1824–1907), later 1st Baron Kelvin of Largs, made many important scientific discoveries and counted Joule and Faraday among his collaborators. In 1849 he introduced the absolute scale of temperature that defined absolute zero (-273° Celcius) as the point at which gaseous molecules cease all motion. Kelvin also paved the way for the computer, inventing a pulley-driven machine in 1879 that operated using Boole's binary principles. Kelvin's invention was capable of making rudimentary mathematical calculations, for example forecasting tidal patterns. The first reliable working version of the machine was constructed in 1930 at the Massachusetts Institute of Technology. He was knighted in 1866 for his role in laying the first cable across the Atlantic and was elevated to the peerage twenty-six years later. The kilowatt hour is also sometimes called the Kelvin.

Kepler's laws

German astronomer Johannes Kepler (1571–1630) defined the three laws of planetary motion, among which was the proposition that the planets orbit in an ellipse around the sun. This work was to have an important influence on Isaac Newton's gravitational theories and remains a milestone in modern astronomy. Kepler's early studies came to the attention of important astronomers such as Galileo and Tycho Brahe, the imperial mathematician for the Holy Roman Empire. Kepler first postulated his theories while working at Brahe's observatory near Prague and succeeded his employer as court mathematician on the latter's death in 1601.

Keynesian

Proposition that a planned economy with a measure of public control is neccessary within the capitalist system. The Great Depression destroyed conventional economic wisdom that the free market alone could bring about prosperity. John Maynard Keynes, 1st Baron Keynes of Tilton (1883–1946), advocated planned intervention to stimulate demand and ultimately raise the standard of living. Like the policies of Malthus and Adam Smith, his *Treatise on Money and the General Theory of Employment* (1935–6) revolutionized economic thinking internationally. Keynes thrived both on academia and his association with the libertine Bloomsbury set, which counted Virginia Woolf and E.M. Forster among its protagonists. His bisexuality notwithstanding, he remained happily married to a Russian ballerina. His last great achievement was to negotiate the terms of the US loan to Britain after World War II, by which time he had joined the governors of the Bank of England and had been elevated to the peerage.

Kilroy

Drawings of this bald-headed character peering over a wall cropped up across the US towards the end of World War II, accompanied by the words, 'Kilroy was here'. The phrase was said to have been scrawled by a military equipment inspector at Quincy, Massachusetts, James J. Kilroy, on materials sent all over the world by Air Transport Command. Its origin is alternatively attributed to a Sergeant Francis Kilroy whose name also adorned containers of weapons and supplies. The primitive cartoon face is known by different names in different countries. In Britain he became *Chad*, who commented with bemused detachment on the shortages brought about by rationing; in the Antipodes he was *Foo*.

King Charles spaniel

Short, compact dog with a silky black and white or black and tan coat, domed skull and short muzzle. Samuel Pepys complained that Charles II, the so-called Merry Monarch (1660–85), was more attentive to the spaniels that would come to bear his name than his royal duties. Before and after the Restoration, small spaniels were a favourite at Court. The lapdog of Mary, Queen of Scots, a black and white spaniel, is said to have died two days after her execution 'perhaps from loneliness or grief'. A portrait

of Charles's sister, Henrietta d'Orleans, painted in 1660, shows her cradling in her lap a spaniel wearing earrings.

King Dick

Latterly an insult aimed at the pompous male by casting aspersions on the size of his genitalia, as in: 'Who do you think you are, King Dick?'; historically a derogatory term employing a contraction of the name 'Richard'. The epithet was famously applied to Richard Cromwell (1626–1712), who succeeded his father as Lord Protector of the Puritan Commonwealth in 1658 but showed none of the former's aptitude for office. His involuntary abdication two years later led to the eventual restoration of the monarchy. Cromwell fled to France where he lived as 'John Clarke' for a number of years, before travelling on to Geneva and finally returning to England in 1680, living in seclusion at Cheshunt until his death.

King Edward potato

Oval variety, the full title of which is the King Edward VII. The monarch acceded to the throne on the death of his mother, Queen Victoria, in 1901. The originator of the breed is unknown but it was introduced in 1902 by J. Butler of Lincolnshire. It is very susceptible to blight. Butler also introduced the King George V potato in 1911.

King James Bible

Standard version of the Bible for the English-speaking world from its publication in 1611 to the mid-twentieth century; more correctly the Authorized Version. Forty-seven scholars began work on a new translation of the Bible in 1607 on the order of James I (1550–1625, ruler between 1603–25). Latterly the King James Bible has been superseded by the Revised Standard Version (US 1946–52), New International Version (US 1965–73) and the New English Bible (UK 1970), but its phraseology remains an influence on language and literature.

Knickerbockers

Baggy trousers fastened below the knee. The word first appears in print as the name of the author of Washington Irving's pseudonymous *Knickerbocker's History of New York* (1809), a satire purporting to tell the story of Dutch settlement in the city. Characters wearing baggy breeches were depicted in the illustrations by George Cruikshank. The word entered common parlance in the mid-nineteenth century; and the article of dress became fashionable among the shooting and country fraternity in the UK from the 1860s onwards. Its contraction, 'knickers', referring to women's loose drawers, dates from the 1880s.

Laconic

Of few words. Laconia was an ancient Greek state in the Pelopponnese, the capital of which was Sparta. It differed from its neighbours in eschewing coins and its women enjoyed almost equal status to men. It gained a reputation for terse language when a predatory Philip of Macedon sent a missive that threatened: 'If I invade Laconia I shall turn you out.' The Laconian magistrates replied: 'If.'

Lazar

Beggar; untouchable. From the biblical parable of Lazarus, the leper who lay suffering from his sores at the gate of the selfish, rich man, begging for crumbs from the table. When the two men died, the angels carried Lazarus to heaven. The rich man, Dives, was tormented in hell. A quarantine hospital is sometimes called a **Lazar House** or a **Lazaret**.

Leotard

Close-fitting body stocking resembling the outfit worn by acrobats, popular today among gymnasts, dancers and fitness fanatics. Jules Léotard (1842–70) was the world's first flying

trapeze artiste. He first performed his act at the Cirque Napoleon in Paris in 1859, leaping from one trapeze to the next over the heads of his astounded audience. Léotard soon gained international acclaim in his short career. He died of smallpox, aged 28.

Lesbian

Female homosexual. Lesbos is one of the largest Greek isles in the Aegean Sea and was home to the poet Sappho and her contemporaries in the seventh century BC. Her most famous poems celebrate the love of a woman for another (though there is no specific reference to physical relations).

Leviathan

Immense, of great size. Hebrew name for a sea monster, possibly a crocodile or a whale, which can only be subdued by God. In the Book of Isaiah, it is described as 'Leviathan the gliding serpent … the monster of the sea.' The leviathan is thought to denote chaos; similar legends are found in earlier Babylonian and Canaanite writings. Thomas Hobbes appropriated the term for his famous treatise on the need for a social contract and greater liberalism, *Leviathan, or the Matter, Form, and Power of a Commonwealth, Ecclesiastical and Civil* (1651).

Levi's

Brand of denim jeans; almost a generic term for all jeans since the 1940s. Levi Strauss (1830–1902) travelled across America in 1850 with a wagonload of canvas, which he hoped to convert into tents to sell to miners in the Californian gold rush. Instead he found there was greater demand for the fabric as hard-wearing trousers and overalls. Reinforcing the seams and riveting pockets, Strauss's sturdy work clothes withstood substantial wear and tear and found a ready market. Strauss and his partner J. Davis patented their garments in 1873. It was not until the 1940s that jeans became widely adopted as casual wear.

Libation

Any alcoholic beverage. In Roman mythology, Liber was the god of fertility. He is identified with the Greek deity Dionysus or Bacchus (*see* **bacchanalia**), whose nickname was *Lyaeus*, 'the liberator'. The name originally referred to the wine spilled on the ground of the temple in Graeco-Roman ceremonies as an offering to the gods. Liber's festival, held on 17 March, marked the initiation ceremony for Roman youths who donned adult togas for the first time.

Lilliputian

Small-minded, petty. When Gulliver encountered the tiny people of Lilliput in Jonathan Swift's *Gulliver's Travels* (1721), he found they bore all the same character flaws as their human counterparts.

Linnaean classification

Swedish botanist Carl von Linné or, as he became known, Carolus Linnaeus (1707–78), devised the system by which we classify all creatures in both the plant and animal kingdoms using two Latin names. The genus is always written first, the species second, as in *Homo sapiens*, or 'wise or sapient man'. Linnaeus practised medicine successfully before returning to Uppsala University to become Professor of Medicine, then Chair of Botany, a position he held for the rest of his life. He travelled extensively, cataloguing all then-known organisms, until a stroke severely affected his health. His manuscripts and specimens were brought to London after his death by Sir James Edward Smith, who founded the Linnean Society. The collection resides in Burlington House, London.

Listeria

Genus of bacteria named after the founder of antiseptic surgery, Joseph Lister, 1st Baron Lister of Lyme Regis (1827–1912). The most common species, *Listeria monocytogenes*, can be found in soft foods such as cheese and leads to diseases including meningitis and septicaemia (in which foreign organisms infect the bloodstream). Until the end of the nineteenth century, nearly half of all patients who underwent surgery died from infection. Lister studied Pasteur's (*see* **pasteurization**) work on sterilization and applied his methods to the operating theatre. He used carbolic acid to prevent sepsis and introduced drainage tubes and absorbable ligatures. The result was a revolution in surgery. Lister's success in eliminating germs led to another curious distinction: his name was appropriated by commercial interests and applied to a type of mouthwash. In spite of his strong objections, the name stuck. **Listerine** remains one of the most widely sold brands.

Little Lord Fauntleroy

Precocious young boy. The 1886 novel of the
same name by Manchester-born US author
Frances Hodgson Burnett tells the story of
an American child who inherits an English
earldom. His velvet suit with lace trimmings
was said to have been based on Oscar
Wilde's attire. It was popular with mothers
in the late Victorian age. Children compelled to
wear the ridiculous garb begged to differ.

Lobelia

Genus of plants with red, white, yellow or blue five-lobed flowers,
cultivated in warm climates. Matthias de l'Obel (1538–1616) was
a Flemish botanist and physician to James I.

Lobster Newburg

Main course consisting of lobster meat, egg yolks, cayenne
pepper and cream. When Charles Dickens and other nineteenth-
century worthies passed through New York there was only one
place to dine: the sumptuous Delmonico's restaurant, which also
gave rise to classic creations such as baked Alaska and chicken
à la king (originally à la Keene, in honour of a customer). This
particular dish was supposedly the creation of a West Indian ship's
captain by the name of Ben Wenburg. But when the captain and
the restaurant's owners fell out, the Delmonico brothers subtly
transposed the first and third letters of the dish's name.

Loganberry

Acidic fruit belonging to the blackberry family used in jams, desserts and wine but which many find too tart to eat raw. The trailing, prickly plant, *Rubus longanobaccus*, which bears the loganberry was first cultivated in 1881 by James Harvey Logan (1841–1928), an amateur horticulturalist and superior court judge in Santa Cruz, California.

Lolita

Pubescent girl who is aware of her sexuality. The novel *Lolita* (1957) by Russian writer Vladimir Nabokov tells the story of the middle-aged American, Humbert Humbert, who falls in love with and abducts the thirteen-year-old title character.

Lombard rate

Key German interest rate used by the Bundesbank to set a ceiling on money market rates. The Lombards were an ancient Germanic race who ruled northern Italy between the sixth and eighth centuries, and developed a reputation as money lenders and mercantilists in medieval times. In English, Lombard is a byword for 'banker', from the City of London street which was developed into a major banking centre by Italian financiers.

Lorelei

Siren; temptress. Originally, the name of the large rock jutting out over the Rhine, near St Goar, where a siren's song would lure sailors to their death. The story was made famous by the poem *Die Lorelei* by Heinrich Heine. The legend inspired others including Mendelssohn who used it as the basis of an incomplete opera.

Lothario

Promiscuous male with strong sexual prowess. Originally a 'haughty, gay, gallant' character in *The Fair Penitent* (1703), a tragedy by Nicholas Rowe. A character with a similar name cropped up in *The Cruel Brother* (1630) by Nicholas Davenant, a playwright who hinted that he was the illegitimate son of Shakespeare.

Luddite

Gangs of English labourers who destroyed industrial machinery, fearful of the prospect of unemployment. The Luddite movement took its name from Ned Ludd, purportedly a Leicestershire textile worker who smashed up weaving frames in 1799. Twelve years later, organized protests by the Ludds or Luddites began in earnest in Nottinghamshire and the cause found widespread support in other counties. Initially the gangs operated by stealth and by darkness, but rioting and murder were to follow when employers ignored their concerns. The authorities responded with mass executions and transportation. At the end of the Napoleonic Wars economic recession sparked new protests but the movement petered out in 1816. Today the refusal of people to embrace industrial change and new technology is said to betray a Luddite tendency.

Luger

German handgun invented by Austrian George Luger in 1898. The semi-automatic pistol was made in both 7.76mm and 9mm calibres with a removable magazine in the hand grip. It was deployed for civilian and military use until 1943 and became a regulation weapon in countries including Nazi Germany. Some models were revived in the 1970s.

Lynch

Hanging administered by a mob without recourse to a fair trial. The practice of lynching dates back to the Middle Ages: the origin of the term, first known as 'Lynch's law', is far from certain. In the 1770s or 1780s, a Virginian Captain William Lynch (1742–1820) and his fellow landowners issued a blunt warning to outlaws: 'if they will not desist from their evil practices, we will inflict such corporeal punishment on him or them, as to us shall seem adequate to the crime committed'. But the name of Lynch was already associated with this particular brand of rough justice; about this time another Virginian, Charles Lynch (1736–96), was in the dock for terrorizing political opponents and in the 1760s a band calling itself 'the Regulators' would mete out punishment at Lynche's Creek in South Carolina.

Macadamia nut

Flavoursome, edible fruit of the evergreen *Macadamia integrifolia* and *Macadamia tetraphylla* trees. Macadamias are native to north-eastern Australia and were developed as a successful crop in Hawaii. John Macadam (1827–65) was the secretary of the Philosophical Institute of Victoria, Australia.

Mach number

Scale measuring the speed of an object or fluid, relative to the speed of sound. At Mach 1 an object is travelling at the speed of sound; Mach 2 is twice the speed of sound, etc. Moravian philosopher and physicist Ernst Mach (1838–1916) carried out major research into thermodynamics that was later to help Albert Einstein develop his theory of relativity. He also held that only science that was observable had any meaning and believed atoms were merely hypothetical.

Machiavellian

Opportunistic, scheming and amoral attitude, especially applied to politicians. Florentine statesman Niccolo Machiavelli (1469–1527) both admired and reviled the actions of his master, the cunning Cesare Borgia. He took the dispassionate view that his master's terrorism and amorality had brought prosperity and peace to Florence. So when Cesare was deposed, Machiavelli set out the principles and tactics he believed a strong leader should employ for the betterment of the state and society. *The Prince* (1513), his famous treatise to the new ruler, Lorenzo de' Medici, was so naively frank that it was Machiavelli who gained a reputation for unscrupulousness, rather than the politicians who were putting his theories into practice. He was suspected of plotting against the Medici, tortured and dismissed from office. His status was later restored and Machiavelli died in retirement.

Mackintosh

Raincoat. Charles Macintosh was an industrial chemist in Glasgow who invented new dyeing processes and helped

develop bleaching powder before discovering in 1823 the process for waterproofing fabric with rubber. Macintosh patented his discovery and founded a company in Manchester to manufacture the new garments. They did not meet with universal acclaim until vulcanised rubber, which withstood changes in temperature, came on to the market in 1839. Today, the name 'mackintosh' (sic) or 'mack' refers to any modern plastic raincoat.

Mc or Mac

Prefix denoting inferiority, which owes its origins more to the methods of mass production of McDonald's restaurant meals than the relative merits of the cuisine. The term entered general usage in the 1980s to imply colourful and insubstantial products: the national daily newspaper *USA Today* was derogatively referred to as a 'McNewspaper'. More recently, the relatively low level of youth wages, compared to the rest of industry, led to the introduction of the term 'McJob' to mean any low-paid, low-skill position. It was popularized by the Canadian author Douglas Coupland in *Generation X* (1992). The McDonald's fast food empire was founded by brothers Maurice and Richard McDonald in San Bernardino, California. The chain began its rise to prominence in 1954 when the brothers entered a franchise agreement with mixmaster salesman Ray Kroc. McDonald's serve more than sixty-eight million customers each day.

McCarthyism

Political witch-hunting. As the Cold War took hold, Republican Senator for Wisconsin, Joseph Raymond McCarthy (1909-57), made sensational accusations of Communist infiltration into the State Department in particular, and American institutions such as the film industry in general. The accused were harangued before committee hearings and many were driven from their jobs, even though the senator was unable to furnish hard evidence to back up his claims. Allegations that the State Department was riddled with communists and his attacks on President Eisenhower for inaction were the last straw for many in his own party. McCarthy suffered the ultimate humiliation: he was formally censured by the Senate for conduct unbecoming to the traditions of the chamber. His name remains a byword for reckless character assassination.

McCoy, the real

Authentic. Ironically, the origin of the phrase – if you like, the *real real* McCoy – remains a mystery. A similar term was widely used in Scotland in the 1880s to designate high-quality Scotch whisky and probably travelled across the Atlantic with Scottish immigrants to the US. Another candidate is the original cowboy, Joseph McCoy, who ran longhorn steers from Texas to Kansas. In the 1870s he was shipping out more than half a million cattle a year from the railhead at Abilene. Finally there is Norman Selby (1873-1940), the one-time welterweight boxing champ who fought under the name Charles 'Kid' McCoy. Selby's fights outside the ring were as sensational as his professional bouts: he was married ten times to eight women.

Madeleine

In France, small sponge cakes in the shape of seashells; in Britain, sponge cakes filled with jam and desiccated coconut. Marcel Proust's favourite cakes are made from a simple recipe – flour, eggs and sugar. According to legend, they were first baked in the nineteenth century by Madeleine Paulmier, a pastry cook from Lorraine. The explanation is doubtful: similar cakes had been sold in the district for more than one hundred years.

Mae West

Inflatable life jacket used on US Navy vessels during World War II which was said jokingly to approximate the bust of the famous American actress (1892–1980). West remarked: 'I've been in *Who's Who* and I know what's what, but it's the first time I ever made the dictionary.' She was famed for her risqué humour and in 1935 was the most highly paid actress in America. Yet she never uttered the line, 'Come up and see me sometime', which was famously ascribed to her. The nearest approximation was: 'Why don't you come up and see me?', uttered to a young Cary Grant in *Diamond Lil* (1933).

Magellanic clouds

The two smaller companion galaxies to the Milky Way that can only be seen in the southern hemisphere. They were named in honour of the Portuguese explorer Ferdinand Magellan (1480–1521) whose crew noted them on the first journey round the world. Magellan's voyage across the Pacific disproved the prevailing theory that it would take only a matter of days to travel to the New World. The journey took three months.

Magenta

Brilliant red dye extracted from coal tar which was discovered in 1859 and named in commemoration of the bloody Battle of Magenta, fought in the northern Italian town of the same name that year. The narrow victory by the French and Sardinians over the Austrians was little comfort for the 14,000 dead or missing – nearly one in every ten participants. The town was named for the Roman general and emperor Marcus Maxentius (AD 306-312), whose headquarters were situated at Castra Maxentia.

Maginot line

Barrier across the eastern frontier of France, between Switzerland and Belgium. The concrete fortifications were built between 1929 and 1938 at the behest of the French statesman and Minister for War, André-Louis-René Maginot (1877–1932), essentially to protect the returned territories of Alsace-Lorraine. It contributed in no small measure to a sense of complacency against the threat of German invasion. Unfortunately the line did not extend across the Belgian frontier and was easily breached by the Nazis, who entered France through Belgium in 1940. The phrase **Maginot mentality** is also employed against those who hold to an outdated defence strategy.

Magnolia

Genus of North American trees and shrubs which bear large showy pink, white, purple or yellow flowers. Pierre Magnol (1638–1715) was professor of botany at Montpellier.

Malapropism

Confused combination of words, such as 'under the affluence of alcohol', popularized by the character Mrs Malaprop in Sheridan's play *The Rivals* (1775). The word derives from the French phrase *mal à propos* meaning 'out of place'.

Malthusian

Doom-laden; holding to the belief that overpopulation will inevitably lead to decline. Thomas Robert Malthus (1766–1834), Cambridge academic turned curate in Albury, Surrey, was the first economist to question thoroughly the impact of the world's growing population. He worried that humans were multiplying at such a rate that the earth's resources would be unable to cope. His *Essay on the Principle of Population* argued the only solution was sexual abstinence, and created a storm of controversy when it was published anonymously in 1798.

Mammon

Biblical false god of wealth. In the Book of Luke, Jesus explains that people who are dishonest with money are also incapable of dealing with the riches of faith, declaring: 'Ye cannot serve God and mammon.' Milton and Spenser also use the image to personify the evils which wealth attracts. In Syriac, mammon translates as 'riches'.

Man Friday

Faithful retainer; devoted servant. In Jonathan Swift's *Robinson Crusoe* (1719), the native Friday is saved from a life of savagery by a righteous castaway.

Marathon

Long-distance race covering twenty-six miles (42.195km). In 490 BC a young messenger ran twenty-three miles to Athens to deliver the news of the Greek victory at the Battle of Marathon and promptly expired. Some historians think the runner was Pheidippides, who ran from Athens to Sparta *before* the battle to seek assistance. The marathon race was inaugurated at the 1896 Olympic Games. The distance was set at the London games of 1908 and adopted as the standard in 1928. The town took its name from the Arcadian adventurer, Marathus, who offered himself as a sacrifice to ensure the victory of the brothers of Helen of Troy over the city-state of Attica (which was later to become Athens).

Marcel wave

Method of creating a wave in the hair using curling tongs. The process invented by a French hairdresser, François Marcel Grateau (1852–1956), was so successful that he was able to retire while still in his twenties.

Marigold

Tropical plants that bear yellow or yellow-orange flowers, named in honour of the Virgin Mary and for their distinctive colour. Some people still believe common marigold or *Calendula officinalis* possesses medicinal properties and is an effective cure for chilblains and warts. In antiquity marigold was also used to flavour stews.

Marquess of Queensberry rules

Code of rules for amateur boxing contests first published in 1867 and sponsored by John Sholto Douglas (1844–1900), 8th Marquess of Queensberry. The twelve rules devised by John Graham Chambers, a member of the British Amateur Athletic Club, instituted the three-minute round and the rule allowing fallen opponents ten seconds to get back on their feet. Rule eleven forbids shoes or boots containing springs.

Mars

Fourth planet from the sun, orbiting between the earth and Jupiter; its atmosphere is composed mainly of carbon dioxide and temperatures fall to as low as 125°C. It was named after the Roman god of war who is considered the most important god after Jupiter and equates with the Greek Ares. His love for the goddess of beauty, Venus, was a popular subject in art. Preparations for war and the agricultural year both began in **March**, the first month in the early Roman calendar.

Marshall Plan

Common name for the European Recovery Programme devised in 1947 by US statesman George Catlett Marshall (1880–1959) to provide aid to war-torn Western Europe. Marshall embarked on a military career and became the US Army chief of staff at the outbreak of World War II, directing the raising and training of troops. Under the Truman administration he was appointed to mediate in the war between the Chinese nationalists and communists. On becoming Secretary of State he instituted the Marshall Plan and recognized Israel, among his accomplishments. Truman appointed Marshall Secretary of Defense in readiness for the Korean War. In 1953 he was awarded the Nobel Peace Prize.

Martin

Small bird with a forked tail belonging to the swallow family, named oddly after the patron saint of publicans and reformed alcoholics. The feast day of St Martin (c. AD 400) falls on 11 November, once the date of a pagan feast, which explains the saint's colourful patronage. It is also the time of year when the bird migrates. St Martin was a military officer who stopped at

Amiens to share his cloak with a beggar. At night Christ appeared and the heathen Martin was converted to Christianity. He later became Bishop of Tours and died around AD 400.

Martinet

Stickler for strict discipline, especially in the military scene. French colonel, Jean Marquis de Martinet (d. 1672) was the Inspector General of Infantry during the reign of Louis XIV and the commander of the king's own regiment. His constant drilling of the troops and his own tactical brilliance helped transform France's military from a sinecure for young aristocrats into a disciplined fighting force. A little more training would not have gone amiss. At the siege of Duisburg in the Anglo-Dutch wars Martinet was accidentally shot by his own men.

Martini

Cocktail containing gin and dry vermouth, of disputed etymology. The story goes that the drink was invented by Mr Martinez, a New York barman, and gained its name through the subsequent association with a popular brand of Italian vermouth, Martini and Rossi. Jerry Thomas, barman at the Occidental Hotel in San Francisco, supposedly served the first dry Martini in 1860 but until the turn of the century customers generally preferred their Martinis to be much sweeter than today's drink. The fictional adventures of Ian Fleming's suave spy James Bond are responsible for much of the contemporary popularity of the dry Martini – heavy on the gin – and its reputation for sophistication. Bond preferred his Martini 'shaken, not stirred'.

Masochism

Condition in which pleasure, especially sexual pleasure, is derived from pain, usually self-inflicted; also self-defeatism. The nineteenth-century Austrian novelist Leopold von Sacher-Masoch (1835–95) wrote extensively on this theme, the term being coined by the German neurologist Baron Richard von Kraft-Ebing. Sado-masochism is a combination of sadism and masochism.

Mason-Dixon line

The boundary that separates the northern and southern states of America and once denoted the free and slave-owning states. English surveyors Charles Mason (1730–87) and Jeremiah Dixon (d. 1777) were engaged to settle an eighty-year-old border dispute between Pennsylvania and Maryland. Their efforts, begun in 1763, ended four years later, 224 miles west of the Delaware River where hostile Indians forced them to turn back. Mason's valuable survey documents went missing until 1860, when they were rescued from a rubbish tip in Nova Scotia. Little is known of Dixon, other than his appointment as an assistant at Greenwich Observatory and his subsequent travels to the Cape of Good Hope to observe planetary transits.

Mata Hari

Epithet applied to *femmes fatales* and women guilty of betrayal. Mata Hari was the stage name of the Dutch exotic dancer and courtesan Margaretha Geertruida Zelle (1876–1917) and translates from the Malay as 'eye of the day'. She found fame throughout Europe and attracted the favours of senior military officers and government officials from both sides during World War I.

In 1917 she was arrested by the French for passing secrets to a German intelligence officer; one judge accused her of causing 'the death perhaps of fifty thousand of our men'. She protested her innocence to the end, claiming that she had passed on outdated information in order to elicit German secrets to aid the Allies. Mata Hari was executed. The prosecutor, André Mornet, later admitted that 'there was not enough evidence to whip a cat'. The last surviving member of the twelve-man firing squad, Maurice Halbin, was awarded the Legion d'honneur in 1995. 'Smiling, she refused to wear a blindfold,' Halbin recalled, aged 97. 'Then she made a little sign to us with her hand. We fired. I believed, I hope, that I had the only blank bullet in the firing squad.'

Maudlin

Sad, sentimentally drunk. The penitent prostitute St Mary Magdalene was popularly depicted weeping tears of remorse. The same contracted pronunciation applies to Magdalene Colleges at Oxford and Cambridge universities; however, a Magdalene, at one time the name of refuges for fallen women, is pronounced phonetically.

Mauser

Commonly a German military pistol, originally a repeating rifle developed by the German armaments firm founded by brothers Peter Paul (1838–1914) and Wilhelm Mauser (1834–82). The Mausers' initial attempts at weapons design in the 1860s proved unsuccessful until their breech-loading rifle was adopted for use by the Prussian Army in 1884. Their subsequent design became the first magazine rifle, capable of repeated firing without having to be reloaded. The rifle and the modified Mauser Military

Pistol introduced in 1896, were used by German troops in both world wars, but in spite of its success the latter never became the standard service arm.

Mausoleum

Large tomb. The tomb of Mausolus, the ruler of Caria in Asia Minor, was one of the Seven Wonders of the Ancient World. Work on the monument at Halicarnassus began on his death in 353 BC at the behest of Artesmisia, the monarch's widow and sister. It was completed three years later but torn down by Alexander the Great in 334 BC. Some relics survive in the British Museum. Caria was ostensibly a Persian dominion but Mausolus was an expansionist ruler who successfully claimed Greek islands, including Rhodes, and coastal states.

Maverick

Independent-minded person or animal, one who does not follow convention. Texas cattle-rancher Samuel Augustus Maverick (1803–70) allowed his unbranded stock to run free on a 300,000-acre property. Chances are if you came across a cow without a distinguishing mark it was Maverick's. The term came to refer to all renegade creatures and, from the 1880s, was applied to politicians who defied their party leaders. Maverick, with Davy Crockett and Jim Bowie, was a prominent voice in the movement for the secession of Texas from Mexico.

Maxim

Maine-born Sir Hiram Stevens Maxim (1840–1916) invented the first fully automatic machine gun which relied not on a hand-crank but the recoil to eject, load and fire cartridges at a rate of ten shots per second. He first demonstrated the weapon at his London workshop in 1884 and then to an impressive range of visitors, including the Prince of Wales. But sales did not take off until 1914, due in part to a campaign of sabotage by Maxim's rivals (ironically, later to become his partners). In his memoir he recalled one English captain who moaned that the gun was 'ugly as compared to the graceful form of existing guns'. Yet when war broke out both Britain and Germany were using machines based on his patents. Before leaving for Britain, Maxim had a varied career in North America working as a carriage-maker, prize fighter and chief engineer to the first electric light company in the US. Maxim was knighted in 1901.

Maxwell

Unit of magnetic flux, the symbol for which is 'Mx'. The lifelong studies of Edinburgh natural philosopher and astronomer James Clerk Maxwell (1831–79), a contemporary of Isaac Newton, laid the foundations for modern communications. His *Treatise on Electricity and Magnetism* (1873) suggested that electric currents produced electromagnetic waves which operated on a range of frequencies, and forecast that one day it should be possible to communicate using such waves without the need for a conductor wire between two points. Heinrich Hertz verified Maxwell's theories of electromagnetic conductivity in 1885.

May

The fifth month is dedicated to the Roman goddess of spring and fertility, Maia, who was the mother of Mercury.

Mayonnaise

Creamy cold sauce containing the basic ingredients of egg yolks, oil and vinegar. It is suggested the Duc de Richielieu whipped up this concoction when his troops made a victorious landing at Mahon in Minorca in 1756; apparently the ingredients were the only food that the duke could find. This may explain the original French name of the dish, *mahonnaise*. It is equally probable that the word is derived from the old French for 'egg yolk', *moyeu*, or even the verb *manier*, meaning 'to stir'.

Melba toast

Small squares of thin toasted bread named after the Australian soprano, Dame Nellie Melba, real name Helen Armstrong (1861–1931). Melba made her operatic debut in 1887 and took her stage name from her home city of Melbourne. She performed in all the major opera houses of the world, returning to Australia in 1927. Repeated announcements of her impending retirement and a seemingly neverending series of farewell concerts sorely tested the patience of her public. In Australian parlance 'to do a Melba' means to engage in a prolonged farewell. Her name also adorns **Peach Melba**, a dessert consisting of peaches, vanilla ice cream and raspberry purée.

Mendelevium (Md)

Chemical element, atomic number 101. Dimitri Ivanovich Mendeleev (1834–1907) was a Russian chemist and educationalist who devised the periodic table as we know it. In 1869 he surmised that if the elements were arranged in the order of their atomic weights it would therefore be possible to forecast the existence of elements that had not yet been discovered and the properties of their compounds. Mendeleev's discovery brought international fame and honours but his testy manner was frowned upon by Russia's Imperial Academy of Sciences who never recognized him.

Mentor

Person, usually older, from whom one seeks wise counsel or guidance. In Greek mythology Mentor was an old friend of Odysseus who acted as an adviser to his son, Telemachus. On the fall of Troy, the goddess of wisdom Athena assumed the guise of Mentor, accompanying Telemachus on his quest for his father.

Mephistophelean

Devilishly clever, cunning and contemptuous. In the medieval tale of man's temptation, Faust agrees to sell his soul to Mephistopheles, an incarnation of the devil, but eventually outwits the demon. The story has captured the imagination, so to speak, of successive generations of writers. Notable retellings include *Dr Faustus* by Christopher Marlow (1604) and Thomas Mann (1947).

Mercator projection

Method of drawing maps in which the lines of latitude and longitude are at right angles to each other, making navigating easier. Gerhard Kremer, whose name latinized is Gerardus Mercator (1512–94), was a manufacturer of mathematical instruments and was hounded from Flanders for his Protestant beliefs. Mercator settled in Germany where he devoted himself to the study of cartography and issued his new-look map of the world in 1568.

Mercury

Planet closest to the sun with no atmosphere and a temperature during the day of 400°C; silvery-white chemical element, the symbol for which is 'Hg'. Mercury was the Roman god of science and eloquence (the Greek equivalent was Hermes). He was a messenger for his father, Jupiter, and is usually depicted as a young man wearing a winged hat and shoes and carrying a staff around which are entwined two snakes. The word **mercurial** refers to one with an agile mind or light-hearted in spirit. The element was so named because of its perceived quickness of movement.

Mesmerize

Hypnotize; latterly to astound. Austrian physician Franz Anton Mesmer (1734–1815) was an early exponent of hypnosis as therapy. He believed that his group sessions in the form of seances would transmit healing powers or 'animal magnetism' to his patients. But his medical colleagues accused him of witchcraft and Mesmer was forced to flee Vienna for Paris where he met with similar scepticism. Louis XVI appointed a commission of investigation that dismissed Mesmer's methods as quackery. He lived out his final days in London. Other doctors were more open to new ideas and Mesmer's work precipitated serious study of hypnotism later in the nineteenth century to treat medical and psychiatric conditions.

Messerschmitt

German aircraft invented by Willy Emil Messerschmitt (1898–1978). Enthralled by the prospect of flight from his days at technical college in Bamburg, Messerschmitt built gliders, one of which achieved an unofficial world record for the length of time it could stay airborne. He soon graduated to aircraft design and, when the Nazi party came to power, entered a secret competition to invent the aeroplanes that would re-equip the Luftwaffe. His design, *Me109*, became the Germans' standard fighter during World War II. By 1944, his factory was turning out 2,000 a month in addition to bombers and transport carriers. Arrested and imprisoned at the end of the war, Messerschmitt returned to his chosen field in Spain in 1952 and later was free to resume work at home. The firm that he co-founded is today Germany's largest aerospace company, building missiles, transport systems and civilian and military aircraft.

Messier numbers

Catalogue of 103 star clusters and nebulae identified by French astronomer Charles Messier (1730–1817). His original intention was to compile a list of cellestial objects that could easily be confused with comets, Messier's primary interest. He published his first catalogue in 1711, listing the Crab Nebula as M1. Others added to the list, which was largely rendered obsolete by the New General Catalogue issued in the nineteenth century. However, in some instances the familiar Messier numbers still apply.

Methuselah

Aged person so called after the oldest man in the Bible. Methuselah, son of Enoch, lived 969 years according to the Book of Genesis and was still fathering children well into his seventh century.

Micawber

Eternal optimist, in spite of constant failure. The character of Wilkins Micawber in Charles Dickens' *David Copperfield* (1850) was undaunted by the lack of success of his business ventures but continued to hold out hope that the next scheme would make his fortune. He made no provision for the future and was constantly in debt. Micawber finally left for Australia to take up a post as a magistrate.

Mickey Finn

An alcoholic drink that has been drugged, usually with the intention of robbing the unconscious victim. The term is ascribed to a notorious nineteenth-century Chicago innkeeper of the same name who would spike the drinks of his patrons. Chlorine was particularly effective, inducing an anaesthetic state when mixed with water.

Mickey Mouse

Anything trivial or inferior. The famous cartoon mouse, originally called Mortimer, starred in his first animated short feature in the 1920s. He earned his creator, Walt Disney, a special Academy Award in 1932 and remains the symbol of the anything but trivial communications conglomerate which still bears Disney's name.

Midas touch

One who succeeds in all endeavours, especially in business, is said to have the Midas touch. The cautionary tale of the Phrygian king warned the ancient Greeks of the evils of greed. Granted a wish by Dionysius, Midas requested the power to turn everything into gold. Delight turned to distress when even his food became transformed and the foolish king begged to have the gift withdrawn. The penitent Midas was forced to bathe in the Pactolus River, where gold was later found in its sand.

Mills bomb

Serrated, oval hand grenade employed by the Allies in World War I. English engineer, Sir William Mills (1856–1932) established Britain's first aluminium foundry and manufactured components for early automobiles and aeroplanes. In 1915 he built a munitions works in Birmingham to produce the new high-explosive grenades, the most reliable yet invented. A grateful government rewarded Mills with a knighthood and a not inconsiderable £27,750. Mills fought a celebrated legal case, insisting he was not liable for taxation on the amount. The courts disagreed and he was forced to pay up.

Mnemonic

Rhyme or similar device to aid one's memory, such as 'i before e, except after c'. Psychologists say the more abstract the device, the greater likelihood the knowledge will be retained. Mnemosyne was the Greek goddess of memory, the daughter of Uranus (heaven) and Gaea (earth). She was also the mother, by Zeus, of the nine Muses.

Moebius strip

Strip of paper, one end of which has been twisted 180 degrees before attaching it to the other, forming a continuous surface with only one side and one edge. German mathematician August Ferdinand Moebius (1790–1864) made important contributions to the disciplines of geometry and astronomy but it was this discovery in the field of topology, presented in a paper found after his death, for which he is best known today. Moebius used the strip of paper to illustrate the properties of one-sided surfaces. A contemporary, Johann Benedict Listing, made the same discovery independent of Moebius.

Molly

Brightly coloured freshwater fish of the genus *Mollienisia*, found in tropical and subtropical waters of America. The salt water, mainly herbivorous, fish were named in honour of French statesman Comte Nicolas-François Mollien (1758–1850), who earned Napoleon's gratitude for improving the efficiency of the public treasury.

Molotov cocktail

Simple petrol bomb consisting of a bottle filled with flammable liquid and a long fuse. When thrown against its target, the bottle bursts and the flames spread. It was invented by the Finns who were protesting against Russian manoeuvres in 1940 and named after Vyacheslav Mikhailovich Skryabin, alias Molotov (1890–1986), the Russian foreign minister at the time. Molotov was a staunch supporter of Stalin who negotiated the non-aggression pact between the Soviet Union and Nazi Germany in 1939 and later took part in the Allies' preparations for peace at Yalta. Molotov was expelled from the

Communist Party for his role in trying to depose Khruschev and reinstated only at the age of nintey-four. Molotov cocktails are still commonly used in violent street protests around the globe.

Montessori method

Educational system that offers children the chance to develop at their own rate in a controlled environment. Italian educator Maria Montessori (1870–1952) introduced her methods in a school for disabled children in Rome, allowing students a greater measure of independence and capacity for self-motivation. The results of her experiments were so encouraging that the teaching system was extended to regular students and Montessori undertook to promote her methods throughout the world. However, her success corresponded with the rise of Mussolini, forcing her to leave Italy and eventually settle in the Netherlands.

Montezuma's revenge

Euphemism for diarrhoea, usually but not exclusively associated with US visitors to Mexico. Montezuma II (1466–1520) was the Aztec emperor imprisoned by the conquistadors and killed by his own subjects when he commanded them to submit to Cortez. Other imaginative variations include the Aztec two-step, Mexican foxtrot, Delhi belly and Bali belly.

Moog synthesizer

Electronic keyboard that can artificially reproduce musical sounds. US engineer Robert Arthur Moog (1934–2005) began work on electronic instruments in the 1950s. He had produced five models by 1962, patenting the device for commercial use in

1965. It was his collaboration with composers Harry Deutsch and Walter Carlos that popularized the instrument; Carlos's 1969 album *Switched On Bach* became an international bestseller. With further developments in the 1970s, synthesizers were able to produce a wider range of sounds. Popular musicians particularly became enamoured of the smaller, portable versions.

Morphine

Narcotic painkiller extracted from opium. The winged god of dreams, Morpheus, revealed himself in human form while people slept. His father, Hypnus, was the Greek god of sleep. The addictive drug was a favourite of dissolute literary figures as well as the fictional detective Sherlock Holmes, who administered a dosage in a seven per cent solution.

Morse code

International telegraph code. Samuel Finley Breese Morse (1791–1872) was an artist well into his forties, studying painting in Britain, France and Italy, when he became fascinated by the early electrical demonstrations. He devised a crude system for transmitting electrical impulses over wire in 1843, basing his efforts on the work of earlier British pioneers William Cooke and Charles Wheatstone and Princeton scholar Professor Joseph Henry. However, the distinctive code of dots and dashes was the creation of Alfred Vail, a telegraph enthusiast and the son of Morse's benefactor. Morse began commercial operations in 1845. The first message read 'Everything worked well'; the first commercial transmission was the now-famous line 'What hath God wrought?' devised not by Morse but the daughter of the then Commissioner of Patents. Morse was also among the first

American photographers and, disturbingly, a passionate advocate of slavery and anti-Catholicism.

Mrs Peasgood's

Popular type of large baking apple, more correctly known as Peasgood's Nonsuch. The variety was introduced in the 1850s by a Mrs Peasgood from Grantham, Lincolnshire.

Münchhausen's syndrome

Medical disorder in which the sufferer invents non-existent symptoms. German soldier, Karl Friedrich Hieronymous von Münchhausen (1720–97), was renowned for the exaggerated versions of his exploits. At his estate in Bodenwerder he regaled visitors with his impossible tales and published seventeen of his stories in Germany between 1781 and 1783. The books were an inspiration to other writers and proved so popular that an English-language edition, *Baron Münchhausen's Narrative of his Marvellous Travels and Campaigns in Russia*, compiled by Rodolf Erich Raspe, appeared two years later.

Murphy bed

Foldaway beds concealed in cupboards, invented by American manufacturer William Laurence Murphy (1876–1950). Murphy beds were once a common feature of small flats, notably in the US. They have largely been superseded by the sofabed.

Namby-pamby

Insipid, cloyingly sentimental. Originally the nickname of the English poet Ambrose Philips (1674–1749) whose wishy-washy verse was derided by his contemporaries. The dramatist Henry Carey bestowed the name after a particularly gushing series of pastorals which Philips had addressed to the children of Lord Carteret. Pope wrote, 'He used to write Verses on Infants, in a strang Stile, which Dean Swift calls the Namby Pamby Stile.'

Narcissus

Vain person; genus name for flowers including the daffodil and jonquil. In Greek mythology, Narcissus was an attractive youth who spurned the love of the gods and the spirits. Instead he became enamoured of his own reflection in a pool and drowned when he tried to embrace it. When the nymphs attempted to retrieve his body they found only a flower. **Narcissism** is defined as excessive admiration for oneself.

Nebuchadnezzar

Large bottle of champagne, holding the equivalent of twenty normal bottles. In the Books of Jeremiah and Daniel, the tyrannous Babylonian king (605–562 BC) destroyed the temple at Jerusalem and enslaved the Jewish people in Babylon. He was punished for his arrogance by going insane and lived out his final days grazing in a field. To 'take Nebuchadnezzar out of the grass' is a euphemism for withdrawal after sexual intercourse.

Nemesis

One's worst enemy. Nemesis was the Greek goddess of retribution who exacted punishment on evil-doers and people afflicted with excessive self-pride or arrogance. She is said to have been responsible for inciting the wealthy Croesus (*see* **Croesus, rich as**) to mount his last ruinous campaign against the Persian emperor, Cyrus. Nemesis was also capable of assuming various guises and in some legends transformed herself into the swan, from whose egg hatched Helen of Troy.

Neptune

Far-flung planet situated between Uranus and Pluto, with a surface temperature of a chilly -200°C. Neptune was the Roman god of fresh water, later of the sea. Like his Greek equivalent, Poseidon, Neptune is portrayed in art holding a trident and accompanied by a dolphin. He also gives his name to the artificially produced chemical element, **neptunium (np)**, atomic number 93.

Newton (N)

Unit of physical force, defined as the force required to accelerate one kilogram by one metre per second per second. Isaac Newton (1642–1727) was the premier scientist of the rational age, remembered principally for calculating the law of gravity, the three laws of motion and the spectral composition of light. He was also involved in the reform of the currency, had a parliamentary career and tinkered with alchemy. He once brazenly predicted that in the future people would travel at speeds of up to 50 miles per hour. The story of the falling apple precipitating Newton's work on gravitation comes from Voltaire, who obtained the details from one of Newton's relatives. His epitaph, composed by Alexander Pope, sums up his influence: 'Nature and Nature's laws lay hid in night: God said, "Let Newton be", and all was light.'

Nicotine

Resin obtained from leaves of the tobacco plant, *Nicotiana tabacum*. Diplomat Jacques Nicot (1530–1600), introduced the tobacco plant to France, sending the first seeds to Paris in 1550. There are sixty-seven species of tobacco plants, found in America, Africa and Australasia.

Nightingale ward

Hospital ward with two rows of beds and an observation position for the duty nurse. Born in Florence, Italy, Florence Nightingale (1820–1910) sailed with thirty-eight fellow nurses in 1854 to tend to the British wounded in the Crimean War. The ministrations of 'the Lady with the Lamp' were lionized by Victorian society and brought about major reform of hospital nursing and nurses' training. Her name is sometimes invoked to describe a person who provides comfort to another; a **nightingale** is also an old term for a flannel wrap used to keep patients' arms and shoulders from the cold.

Nike

Brand of sports shoes; US ground-to-air missile, named after the Greek goddess of victory. Statues dedicated to Nike were erected to commemorate military gains. The Winged Victory or Nike of Samothrace can be found in the Louvre in Paris. She can also be viewed in various poses on the Acropolis in Athens.

Nissen hut

Semi-cylindrical shelter made of corrugated iron on a cement floor, used chiefly for temporary accommodation during World War II. The building was invented by a Canadian, Lieutenant-Colonel Peter Nissen (1871–30), who served in the British Army during the First World War. The first Nissen hut was built on the Western Front and used as a troop shelter and equipment depot.

Nobel prize

Annual awards for human achievement in the disciplines of physics, chemistry, medicine, literature, economics and peace, funded from the legacy of Alfred Bernhard Nobel (1833–96), the Swedish chemist who invented dynamite. A further award for economics was instituted in 1968 by the Bank of Sweden. Nobel strove to make explosives safer to handle after an accident at his factory killed five people, including his brother Emil. The new product added an earthy compound to the unstable and gelatinous nitroglycerine and was first marketed as Nobel's Safety Powder in 1867. Dynamite was originally intended for use in civil engineering and Nobel, perhaps naively, believed his continuing developments in explosives would one day put a stop to warfare. The first Nobel prizes were awarded in Stockholm in 1901. Each year seven separate committees select a list of nominees, announcing towards the end of the year those who 'have conferred the greatest benefit on mankind'. The chemical element **nobelium** (No), atomic number 102, was discovered in the US in 1958 and named in memory of Alfred Nobel.

Nosey parker

Excessively inquisitive person; one who 'pokes their nose' into the affairs of others. Matthew Parker (1504–75), a sixteenth-century vicar and later Archbishop of Canterbury, was a prime mover in the establishment of the Church of England, earning the enmity of religious opponents. He was also noted for the length of his nose. The epithet has been applied to countless others with a prominent proboscis, not least the Duke of Wellington and Oliver Cromwell.

Ockam's razor

The proposition that unneccessary facts should be eliminated in the style of dissection by razor in order to properly analyze a subject, also called the Law of Economy. William of Occam (1285– c. 1349), a Franciscan philosopher and theologian, employed this rule sharply.

Odyssey

Journey, quest for knowledge or wisdom. Homer's epic poem, *The Odyssey*, follows the ten-year adventures of Odysseus (also known as Ulysses) in the Trojan War and his eventual return home to Ithaca.

Oedipus complex

Psychological description of a son's erotic attraction to his mother and corresponding hatred of his father. The condition was termed by Sigmund Freud, after the story by Sophocles. Oedipus was a Theban king who unwittingly killed his father, Laius, in a quarrel and subsequently married his mother, Jocasta, and sired four children. When Oedipus discovered the truth, he tore his eyes out and abdicated the throne.

Oersted

Unit measuring the strength of a magnetic field, or magnetic intensity, represented by the symbol 'Oe'. Danish physicist Hans Christian Oersted (1777–1851) was the first man to show a direct link between electricity and magnetism – and all by accident. During a lecture in Copenhagen, Oersted placed a wire carrying an electric current next to a magnetic needle. The needle moved, demonstrating the process known as electromagnetic induction. His serendipitous experiment led directly to Ampère's work on electromagnetism. Five years later, Oersted also became the first person to extract aluminium from bauxite.

Ogre

Monster. Thought to be a variation of Orcus, another name for Pluto (the Roman Hades), the ruler of the dead. The word first appeared in 1697 in a book by Perault, *Histoires ou contes du temps passé,* to describe unpleasant giants who thrived on human flesh.

Ohm (Ω)

Unit of electrical resistance; the term was adopted in 1881. German physicist Georg Simon Ohm (1789–1854) devised the mathematical calculation for the law of the flow of electricity. His work was only recognized later in his life and received more acclaim internationally than at home. An **ohmmeter** measures the amount of electrical resistance in ohms.

OK

Signifying understanding; a correct state of affairs. With 'gone for a Burton' (*see* **Burton, gone for a**), perhaps the most contentious of all eponyms. The many and varied explanations may account for its rapid adoption into the lexicon throughout the nineteenth century. They include: 'orl korrect'; 'Old Kinderhook', hometown nickname for US President Martin Van Buren during the election campaign of 1840; Aux Kayes, a Haitian port; 'oikea', a Finnish word for correct; Onslow and Kilbracken, two British lords who initialled bills; the Scottish 'och aye', etc.

Old Bill

Nickname for the police, derived in part from an impotent former figure of authority in cartoon books hugely popular during World War I. Cartoonist and journalist Bruce Bairnsfather portrayed Old Bill as a long-suffering military buffer with a walrus moustache. The character is best remembered for the tagline delivered to a colleague while in a shell crater under heavy bombardment: 'If you know a better 'ole, go to it.' Police magistrates had come to be known as 'beaks' from as early as the sixteenth century; following a logical train of thought, 'beak' became 'bill'.

Olympian

Superior, majestic. Olympus was the mountain home of the ancient Greek gods, led by Zeus. The valley of Olympia in Peloponnese was the site of the original Olympic Games, contested by the ancient Greeks between 776 BC and AD 392. The games were revived as a modern sporting contest between nations in 1896.

Onanism

Masturbation. In the Book of Genesis Onan was ordered to bed his late brother's widow but 'he spilled his semen on the ground to keep from producing offspring'. Onan's punishment by God for his behaviour was death.

Oracle

Infallible source of knowledge. The oracles of ancient Greece were priests or priestesses through whom the gods foretold the future. People would consult the oracles to discover their destiny. Among the most renowned was the oracle of Apollo at Delphi (or the Delphic Oracle) on Mount Parnassus. The word oracle also describes their utterances. Originally from the Latin, *orare*, meaning to speak or pray.

Orangemen

Members of the Orange Order in Northern Ireland which pledges to 'maintain the Protestant Constitution and to defend the King and his heirs as long as they maintain the Protestant ascendancy'. The order was founded in 1795 to commemorate the centenary of the military victory of Dutch-born William of

Orange or William III (1650–1702) over the Catholic James II at the Battle of the Boyne. The King of England from 1689 to 1702 acquired his territorial name through marriage, from the ancient town of Arausio on the Rhône. The House of Orange still rules in the Netherlands.

Orwellian

Dystopian future or sinister state, as described in George Orwell's *Nineteen Eighty-four* (1949). The book's hero, Winston Smith, is subjected to torture for daring to possess independent thought in a permanently warring totalitarian state. Orwell, real name Eric Arthur Blair (1903–50), advocated socialism but was dismayed by its implementation, especially in Russia. His other great work, *Animal Farm* (1945), was a barely disguised fable about Stalin's brutal subjugation of his own people.

Oscar

Film industry awards distributed annually by the US Academy of Motion Picture Arts and Sciences since 1929. There are two versions of the story. Academy librarian Margaret Herrick was supposed to have remarked in 1931 that the golden statuette reminded her of her uncle, Oscar Pierce. The second refers to a throwaway line by Oscar Wilde. Asked if he had won a poetry prize he replied, 'While many people have won the Newdigate, it is seldom that the Newdigate gets an Oscar.' With this in mind, the playwright Charles MacArthur remarked to his wife, the actress Helen Hayes, 'I see you've won an Oscar.' The distinctive statuettes were designed by MGM art director Cedric Gibbons.

Paean

Song of praise, exultation. In Homer's *Iliad*, Paian is described as the god of healing, or the physician to the gods. The title is usually bestowed on Apollo for his ability to bring about victory. The practice of singing hymns or paeans to Apollo is thought to have originated in the seventh century BC; later paeans were sung to other gods.

Paget's disease

The most common bone disease in the world causes a thickening of the bones in the limbs, spine and the skull in older people. It produces severe pain and there is no known cure. Sir James Paget (1814–99), the eminent Victorian doctor, first identified the symptoms in 1876. He later became surgeon to Queen Victoria. It is estimated 600,000 people in England alone suffer from the disease, also known by its Latin name *osteosis deformans*. A second disease, an inflammation of the nipple betraying an underlying cancer of the breast, also bears Paget's name.

Palladian

Neoclassical architectural style that has been both widely popular and influential since the sixteenth century. Renaissance Italian architect Andreas Palladio (1508–80), originally Andrea de Pietro della Gondola, appropriated the clean, rational symmetry of first century AD Roman design to great effect, building palaces, villas and churches in Vicenza and Venice. The translation into English of his *Four Books of Architecture* (1570) nearly 150 years later, led to a major revival of the style. Proponents of Palladianism included Inigo Jones and the US statesman Thomas Jefferson. One of the architect's early patrons, Count Gian Giorgio Trissino, gave Palladio his adopted name, in reference to the deity Pallas Athena, one of the Titans and the father of Nike.

Palladium

Safeguard; something on which to depend for protection. The word may be more commonly associated with the names of concert halls and cinemas today but the original Palladium was a statue with magical powers, carved by a grieving Athena who had slayed her childhood friend, the goddess Pallas. The Trojans believed it granted them divine protection. The fate of the statue is unknown; some say the Greeks took the statue during the sack of Troy; others believe the Palladium was removed to Rome.

Pandora's box

Source of unexpected trouble. In Greek mythology, Pandora was the first woman, created as punishment to Prometheus for giving life to man. Each of the gods bestowed on her gifts that would deliberately bring about man's defeat (hence her name, which derives from the Greek for 'all gifts'). She carried a box or jar containing the world's ills and hope. When her husband opened it, against strict instructions, all the troubles that have come to plague mankind were let loose. Only hope remained.

Panic

Sense of alarm or fear that makes one act without thinking. Half-man, half-goat, Pan was the god of herdsmen. He was generally a peaceful minor Greek deity but easily roused to anger, especially if disturbed during his midday rest or spying upon the nymphs. His unseen presence was supposedly responsible for the strange noises in the forest that spooked travellers, and for the defeat of the fearful Persians at the Battle of Marathon in 490 BC. His name, which means 'all', is said to derive from the delight he gave to the other Olympian gods.

Pants

Trousers; a contraction of pantaloons. In Italian *commedia dell'arte* and, later, English pantomime, Panatoon was the doddering old Venetian who wore baggy trousers. The name is possibly a derivation of St Pantaleone, the patron saint of physicians and popular in Venice when the play was first performed, *c.* 1560.

Paparazzi

Freelance photographers who hunt down notable celebrities and sell their pictures to newspapers and magazines. Paparazzo was a Roman street photographer in pursuit of movie stars in Federico Fellini's film *La Dolce Vita* (1959). The most determined paparazzi go to great lengths to obtain a jump over their rivals, employing telephoto lenses and keeping a retinue of informants such as hotel doormen. Film actors especially have become increasingly wearisome of the invasion of privacy and some have chosen to hit back – often quite literally.

Pap test

Diagnostic test on tissue cells to detect cancer in women. Greek-born physiologist Dr George Nicholas Papanicolaou (1883–1962) discovered that tissue samples observed under a microscope could help to identify the onset of cervical cancer. At New York's Cornell Medical Centre he initiated the simple smear test in which diagnostic samples are taken from vaginal secretions and cells lining the wall of the cervix.

Parkinson's disease

Neurological disorder that usually occurs later in life when sufferers develop a stooped posture and uncontrollable tremors. The symptoms were first observed in 1817 by English surgeon and palaeontologist James Parkinson (1755–1824). He called the disease *paralysis agitans,* but later French neurologist Jean Martin Charcot concluded it was not a form of paralysis at all because muscle control was often well maintained. Whatever it was, Charcot wrote, 'Parkinson's disease' appeared to have no known cause. In the 1950s it was discovered that the disorder was brought about by a lack of a chemical in the brain called dopamine. The drug L-dopa is used to lessen the symptoms but until damaged brain cells can be replaced there remains no known cure.

Parkinson's law

'Work expands to fill the time available for its completion.' The semi-serious theory boosted the reputation of the British author and historian Cyril Northcote Parkinson (1909–93), who based his conclusion on his experiences of bureaucracy while serving in the British Army in Malaya. He had observed that administrators would employ more staff to boost their own prestige. Parkinson's Law was first published in an essay in the *Economist* in 1955.

Pascal

Scientific unit of pressure, equal to one newton (*see* **newton**) per square metre; advanced computer language. French mathematician and philosopher Blaise Pascal (1623–62) demonstrated that air pressure varied depending on altitude. His experiments using tubes containing a column of mercury led to the introduction of the mercury barometer for use in weather forecasting. His work on fluids led him to construct the first syringe and at age nineteen, he built the first calculator, a mechanical device capable of carrying out speedy addition and subtraction by rotating six wheels on the lid of a small box. Before his death, Pascal also helped found public transport, putting together a team of carriages to ply popular routes around the streets of Paris.

Pasteurization

Process of fermentation allowing food and drink to be preserved for longer than normal, using heat to destroy bacteria followed by rapid cooling. French chemist Louis Pasteur (1822–95) stumbled upon his discovery in the 1850s while examining how to extend the storage time of wine. Pasteurization does not allow long-lasting preservation but, because it does not involve cooking, the food retains its flavour. Pasteur also saved the French silk industry from devastation by controlling the disease attacking silkworms, as well as discovering vaccines for diseases including anthrax and rabies. In 1885 he famously saved the life of a young boy who had been bitten by a rabid dog. The boy, Joseph Meister, whose doctor had given him up for dead, was later hired as a gatekeeper at the Pasteur Institute and died in 1940 trying to prevent marauding Nazis from entering Pasteur's crypt.

Pavlova

Antipodean meringue dessert, topped with fruit and cream, named in honour of the Russian prima ballerina Anna Pavlova (1881–1931) while on a tour of Australia and New Zealand in the 1920s. Pavlova danced with both the Imperial Ballet and the Ballet Russes before founding her own company in 1914. She toured extensively with an ever-expanding repertoire and developed a genuine interest in folk dance (she was responsible for reviving the popularity of ethnic dance in India).

Pavlovian

Automatic reflex action conditioned by external stimulus. Russian physiologist Ivan Petrovich Pavlov (1849–1936) demonstrated how behaviour is related to the nervous system by training a dog to associate food with the sound of a bell. Eventually even when only the bell was rung the dog would salivate. Pavlov's work on reflexes followed his studies of the secretions produced by the digestive system, which won him the Nobel Prize for Physiology in 1904. He was an outspoken critic of the Communist system, and, protected by his scientific pre-eminence, dared to stand up to Lenin and Stalin.

Peeping Tom

One who derives sexual gratification from observing others while concealed. The story of Tom the tailor, who peered from his window to gawp at Lady Godiva and was consequently struck blind for his impudence, was added to the story of the naked ride during the reign of Charles II. Godiva was the wife of Leofric, the Earl of Mercia and Lord of Coventry. She undertook the legendary protest in 1040 against the high taxes that her husband had imposed on the citizenry. In response, a mocking Leofric agreed to ease the tax burden if his wife rode naked through the city, which she duly did.

Peter Pan

Eternally youthful person, based on 'the little boy who never grew up' of J.M. Barrie's play (1904) and novel (1911). Peter enlists the help of the three Darling children to travel to Never Never Land to rescue the Lost Boys from the fearsome Captain Hook. At the end of their adventure, the children return to London; all, that is, except Peter who has no wish to grow up. The play was an instant hit on the London stage and Barrie was at the height of his fame. There were some changes to the original draft; the fairy Tinker Bell was to have been called Tippy-Toe.

Peter Principle

'In a hierarchy every employee tends to rise to his level of incompetence'; a dictum advanced by Canadian educationalist Lawrence J. Peter (1919–90) and Raymond Hull (1918–85) in their book, *The Peter Principle* (1966). Peter's pithy observations gained a wide audience. He also proposed that 'if you don't know where you're going, you will probably end up somewhere else'.

Philippic

Bitter denunciation. The Athenian statesman Demosthenes was so incensed by the imperial aggression of Philip of Macedon (382–336 BC) and his son, Alexander the Great, that he used all his oratorical skills to rouse his fearful countrymen to fight for their liberty. They paid little attention; the Athenians sued for peace in 346 BC. Philip despised his eloquent opponent but had less to fear from Athens than his own backyard. He was assassinated by a young Macedonian nobleman. Demosthenes took his own life fourteen years later when Alexander crushed an Athenian revolt.

Philistine

Ignorant or unenlightened person, with little interest in art or thought. The Philistines were a seafaring race who settled in Gaza in the first millennium BC. But their expansionist tendencies led inevitably to battles with the Israelites, as told by the story of Samson in the Book of Judges. They were finally defeated by King David and eventually assimilated with the Semites, who continued to regard their old foes as barbaric. The Philistines also gave their name to the region, which the Greeks dubbed Palestine. The contemporary meaning was popularized by Matthew Arnold in his essay, *Culture and Anarchy* (1869).

Pickwickian

The use of language in a way other than that usually understood. In the opening chapter of Charles Dickens' *Pickwick Papers* (1837), the book's jovial hero employs offensive phrases to denote compliments to his colleague, Mr Blotton. His name, which derives from the utensil used to pull up the wick on an oil lamp, also denotes both a jolly, generous person and a medical syndrome leading to respiratory problems and bulimia in overweight people.

Pilger

To distort or disregard facts in order to advance a political argument, allegedly in the manner of left-wing Australian journalist John Pilger (1939–). The term was coined in the 1980s by the bufferish English writer Auberon Waugh and was at one time employed regularly in his columns in the weekly conservative journal, the *Spectator*. Pilger won international fame for *Year Zero* (1979), his film exposé of the genocidal military regime of the Cambodian communist dictator Pol Pot. Pilger's opponents believe him to be an obsessional conspiracist; his supporters view him as a brave champion of the poor and weak against powerful institutions.

Pinchbeck

Inferior, low quality; an alloy intended to resemble gold and used in cheap jewellery. Fleet Street jeweller Christopher Pinchbeck (1670–1732) concocted the alloy of 83.6 per cent copper and 16.4 per cent zinc initially to make imitation gold watches.

Platonic

Non-physical love between members of the opposite sex. In fact the term derives from attempts by Plato (c. 428–347 BC) in his *Symposium* to define Socrates' interest in young men; he surmised that because the relationships were purely spiritual, it placed them on a higher plane than physical love. The concept was further developed by the Platonic Academy of fifteenth-century Florence. The great Athenian philosopher was originally called Aristocles and was given the name Plato, meaning 'broad shouldered' for his stature or wide brow. His ethical beliefs and his deliberations on society are still an important influence on philosophical thought.

Plimsolls

Rubber-soled sports shoe; canvas deck shoe. English politician Samuel Plimsoll (1824-98) campaigned against unsafe conditions at sea, laying the blame at the feet of the ship owners in his book *Our Seamen* (1872). One of the conditions stipulated by his Merchant Shipping Act of 1876 was a legal limit on the volume of cargo a vessel could hold. The marking on the side of a ship to indicate the correct level of submersion, the load-line, became known as the **Plimsoll Line** or **Plimsoll Mark**. He was called 'the sailor's friend', and gave his name to the footwear worn on boats. Later, rubber-soled shoes became popular on the sportsfield, and they too came to be dubbed plimsolls.

Pluto

The planet farthest from the sun, with a mass one tenth of the earth's surface, was discovered in 1930 by US astronomer Clyde W. Tombaugh. Pluto was a title applied to Hades, the Greek god of the underworld, meaning 'the rich man', for the source of agricultural wealth that the ground delivered. The chemical element **plutonium (Pu)**, atomic number 94, is used in nuclear weapons and as fuel in nuclear power plants.

Pompadour

Hairstyle teased upwards without a parting; purple-pink colour. The Marquise de Pompadour, Jeanne Antoinette Poisson (1721–64), was the wily mistress of Louis XV whose influence extended not only to amorous affairs but political intrigues as well. Her domination of foreign relations saw the reversal of the previous policy of antagonism towards Austria. It led directly to the Seven Years' War that contributed to the decline of France and, inevitably, the monarchy. Pompadour, who met the king when she was twenty-three and took up residence at the Palace of Versailles a year later, left her mark on the fashions of the era. She popularized various items of clothing, including a long fitted coat, her hairstyle and her favourite colour. Several regiments of the British Army adopted the nickname the Saucy Pompadours for the purple coats they wore.

Pontius Pilate

Derogatory name applied to a pawnbroker that presupposes that the terms one is offered are as unfair as the death sentence Pontius Pilate (?–39 AD) brought on Jesus Christ. Pilate was the Roman prefect of Judea (26–36 AD) whose heavy-handed methods offended Jewish sensibilities. His corresponding brutality towards the Samaritans led to his eventual banishment. There are conflicting versions of how Pilate met his end: at his own hands on the orders of Emperor Caligula or as a happy convert to Christianity. The British Army regiment, the First Foot, and later the Royal Scots, were nicknamed **Pontius Pilate's Body-Guards**, in reference to the story in the Book of Matthew. The Jewish priests bribed the bodyguards at Christ's tomb to say they had fallen asleep on the job, so as to conceal the Resurrection. The commander of the First Foot asserted the preeminence of his regiment over a rival French company by insisting that had his men been on duty at the Crucifixion, they would have remained wide awake.

Post toasties

Popular US breakfast cereal. As he underwent treatment at John Harvey Kellogg's Battle Creek sanitarium, it dawned on Charles William Post that there was a fortune to be made in breakfast cereals. He launched a variety of cornflakes under the name Elijah's Manna and laid plans for their export to Britain. But the British Government would not countenance a trademark with such blatant Biblican connotations. The following year Post bowed to pressure and changed the name of the product.

Praline

A sugary confection containing a mixture of almonds or other nuts and caramelized sugar, usually found in boxes of chocolates. The first pralines were supposedly whipped up by Lassagne, the personal chef of French marshal Comte du Plessis-Praslin (1598–1675), but they differed from today's version. They were originally sugar-coated almonds and that definition still applies in France and the southern US.

Priapism

Lewdness; clinical definition of a persistent erection of the penis occurring without sexual arousal. The acute medical condition is usually caused by a blood clot and can occur as a result of damaged nerves or infection. The Greek god of fertility Priapus ensured the success of the harvest. He was the son of Dionysus and Aphrodite and later distinguished by his oversized genitalia and licentous behaviour.

Promethean

Capacity for daring originality. The Greek god Prometheus, whose name translates as 'forethought', disobeyed the orders of his cousin, Zeus, and taught man skills including how to use fire. His punishment was to be chained to a rock for eternity while an eagle ate at his liver; mankind was tormented by the introduction of the first woman, Pandora. Hercules killed the bird of prey and released Prometheus from his fate but the benefactor of mankind was forced forever to carry a chunk of the rock to which he had been chained. In the middle of the eighteenth century a Promethean was a kind of match. The element **promethium** is a radioactive by-product of nuclear fission; its atomic number is 61, the symbol 'Pm'.

Protean

Versatile, capable of taking many forms. The minor deity Proteus tended the herds of sea creatures belonging to Poseidon, the Greek god of the sea. He possessed the power of prophecy but refused to make any revelations to humans. He transformed himself into all manner of creatures to evade capture. He also lends his name to a genus of bacterium called Proteus.

Psyche

The soul, the psychological aspects of one's character. The Greek heroine Psyche was a young woman of such astounding beauty that she scared away all potential suitors. Tired of her spinsterish life, she settled for an existence with a terrible monster who concealed himself at all times. But curiosity got the better of her. Late one night she took an oil lamp and gazed upon his face: her beau was the god of love, Eros (or Cupid). Unfortunately she spilled a drop of hot oil on her lover who awoke and fled. Psyche was captured and enslaved by a jealous Aphrodite but eventually Eros came to her rescue. Their subsequent marriage ensured Psyche's immortality. Psyche translates as 'breath' or 'the soul'. Her depiction in art, with butterfly wings, reinforced the Greek belief that the soul departed the body after death.

Puckish

Impish. The mischievous spirit, Puck, delights in causing mayhem and confusion in William Shakespeare's *A Midsummer Night's Dream* (1595) and is the title character of Rudyard Kipling's *Puck of Pook's Hill*. The hobgoblin, also known as Robin Goodfellow, is of uncertain origin and may have been an Old English variant of the devil.

Pulitzer prize

Prestigious annual awards for US journalism funded from the legacy of the successful Hungarian-born newspaper publisher, Joseph Pulitzer (1847–1911). Prizes are awarded in eight categories: to newspapers, authors, for public service, cartooning, editorial writing, photography news reporting and investigative journalism. Pulitzer built up a stable of colourful newspapers, including the *St Louis Despatch*, but a circulation war in the 1890s with his arch-rival, William Randolph Hearst, took a heavy toll.

Pullman car

Luxurious railway coach. Chicago industrialist George Mortimer Pullman (1831–97) introduced railway sleeper carriages, and his name remains a byword for first-class train travel. The first Pullman car, the Pioneer, began operating in 1859 and its success led to the establishment of the Pullman Palace Car Company, which found a ready international market for its rolling stock. Less glorious was the bloody Pullman Strike, called by local labour unions at the company town in 1894 in response to a twenty-five per cent wage cut. The authorities in Washington responded to industrial action by calling in 2,500 federal troops to break the pickets and set a legal precedent when a court invoked antitrust laws against the strike leaders.

Pyrrhic victory

A victory won at too high a cost. The king of Epirus, Pyrrus or Purrhos (319–272 BC), sought to revive the military glories of his cousin, Alexander the Great, but suffered such great casualties among his troops that it fatally weakened his army and led to its defeat by Rome in 275 BC. At the conclusion of the costly battle of Ausculum in 279 BC, Pyrrus remarked: 'One more such victory over the Romans and we are utterly undone.' He died fittingly fighting the Romans at the battle of Argos in the northern Peloponnese. At the same time as Pyrrus was waging war, the Greek philosopher Pyrrho was establishing the school of sceptical thought, **Pyrrhonism**, which holds that man can only be truly happy when he accepts that he doesn't really understand anything. The war dance of the ancient Greeks, performed in battle dress, was known as the **Pyrrhic Dance**, after its inventor Pyrrichos or for the distinctive fiery-red tunics; the Greek word for fire is *pyro*.

Python

Sub-family of non-venomous snakes which kill their prey by constriction, and are found in Africa, China and South-East Asia. Python was a terrible serpent or dragon which guarded an oracle at Delphi. Apollo slew the beast either to found his own oracle, protected by the priestess Pythia, or because Python had threatened the god's mother, Leto, during her pregnancy. The ancient Greek athletic and musical contest, the Pythian Games, were founded in homage to Apollo's victory. Pytho was an ancient name for Delphi.

Queen Anne legs

These bandy legs weren't attached to Queen Anne (1665–1714) but a style of furniture made popular during the twelve-year reign of Britain and Ireland's last Stuart ruler. The decorative arts of the period did away with much of the ornate styling of the past, paving the way for Palladianism (*see* **Palladian**). The curved legs originated in Chinese porcelain vessels *c.* 1000 BC that were brought back to Europe by the Dutch. The French called them cabriole legs – the legs of a frolicking goat – and it remains the accepted description. The revival of Queen Anne style in the nineteenth century led to a demand among customers for furniture with 'Queen Anne legs'.

Quisling

Traitor, especially a person who betrays one's country. Norwegian fascist politician Vidkun Quisling, originally Abraham Lautitz Jonsson (1887–1945), aided the German occupation of Norway during World War II; he attempted to convert Church and State institutions to the cause of national socialism, earning the enmity of his countrymen. The Nazis rewarded Quisling, who willingly assisted the programme to exterminate the Jews, with the job of puppet Minister President. At war's end he was tried for treason and shot.

Quixotic

Naively idealistic, chivalrous, impractical. Don Quixote, the addled, egotistical knight of Miguel de Cervantes Saavedra's satirical novel of the same name (published in two volumes in 1605 and 1615) read far too many romances for his own good and embarked on a ridiculous quest to set the world to rights. He was accompanied by his stout and sensible squire, Sancho Panza, but throughout their journey Don Quixote's idealism came into stark contrast with the realities of life. The author's profound insights into mankind's own quest opened the book to differing interpretations and ensured its enduring influence.

Raglan sleeves

Diagonal seam from the collar to the underarm, offering more room in the armhole area for garments worn underneath. British general Fitzroy James Henry Somerset, 1st Baron Raglan (1788–1855) wore an overcoat fashioned in such a style during the Crimean War. Raglan lost his right arm at Waterloo, fighting alongside Wellington and later replaced the Iron Duke as the commander of forces. He led the troops in the Crimean War but attracted widespread criticism for mismanaging the campaign. It was Raglan who gave the ill-fated command that led to the disastrous Charge of the Light Brigade in 1854. As Tennyson put it: 'Some one had blundered.' Raglan died of dysentery at Sebastopol before war's end.

Rambo

A macho person who displays aggressive, often violent characteristics. In the novel *First Blood* (1972) by David Morrell, US solider John Rambo returns to Vietnam to rescue compatriots still held captive and exacts bloody revenge on the Viet Cong. The character rose to the status of a national icon on the release of the two films starring muscle-bound actor Sylvester Stallone, *First Blood* (1982) and *Rambo: First Blood 2* (1985).

Lone multiple-killers are invariably depicted in the media as being Rambo-like.

Rastafarian

Pseudo-Judaistic religious sect originating in Jamaica that believes in the divinity of Ethiopian Emperor Haile Selassie (1892-1975), originally Tafari Makonnen. The movement takes its name from the emperor's princely title Ras Tafari. Adherents reject the Caribbean's dominant Christian culture. They hold to the belief that Africans are God's chosen people and that their slavery was God's punishment for wrongdoing. Haile Selassie (meaning 'Might of the Trinity') was crowned emperor in 1930 and did much to modernize Ethiopian society. He was forced into exile by the Italian invasion of 1935 but resumed his rule after the war. Selassie remained in power until a successful military coup was mounted in the year of his death.

Rehoboam

Champagne bottle, traditionally the equivalent of six normal bottles. The autocratic rule of Rehoboam, the son and successor of King Solomon, split greater Israel asunder. Asked at his confirmation ceremony whether he would ease the harsh burden of his father, the new king replied that whereas Solomon had scourged them with whips, he would scourge his people with scorpions. The ten northern tribes needed little prompting to instead unite under the warrior Jeroboam, leaving Rehoboam with the smaller state of Judah, centred on Jerusalem.

Remington rifle

Standard firearms for military and sporting use, constructed by the company founded in 1819 by Eliphalet Remington (1793–1861), a New York barrel-maker. Remington rifles were standard-issue weapons for Union troops in the US Civil War and supplied to the US Government for use in both world wars.

Remington typewriter

First commercially produced typewriter. With the Civil War over, the Remington company diversified into agricultural implements and sewing machines and was looking for other new-fangled products to manufacture. In 1872, Philo Remington (1816–89), the son of the company's founder, was presented with a prototype of the first workable typewriter patented by Milwaukee journalist, printer and politician Christopher Latham Sholes. The firm immediately saw the potential of the new invention but initial sales were disappointing, thanks perhaps to a hefty $125 price tag and poor marketing. The first recipients of typewritten letters, including Queen Victoria, took them to be a gross insult; they thought that the sender was implying they were unable to read. One exception was Mark Twain, an early enthusiast and the first writer to present a typewritten manuscript of a book. By 1878, Remington typewriters included both upper- and lower-case characters and the company began to target office workers and secretaries. At last the invention had found a willing public. At the start of the 1880s, Remington was selling 1,200 typewriters a year, at the end of the decade it was selling that many every month. Unluckily, it was not enough to save the family firm. Expansion coincided with an economic downturn in financial conditions and the Remingtons were forced to sell off their typewriter plant in 1886.

Rhesus factor

The terms Rh positive and Rh negative in blood analysis refer to the presence or absence in the bloodstream of proteins known as antigens, which are capable of producing antibodies to fight disease. The introduction of Rh antibodies into a pregnant woman who is Rh negative, say via a blood transfusion, can lead to complications with the pregnancy and, worst of all, a stillborn child. The Rhesus factor was so-named because similar antigens were found in the blood of the Rhesus monkey of Southern Asia, now known as the *Macaca mulatta*. The Rhesus of antiquity was a warrior who fought alongside the Trojans. Homer records that he was killed by Odysseus and Diomedes, the Thracian king.

Richter scale

Open-ended scale for measuring the intensity of earthquakes, devised by US seismologist Charles Francis Richter (1900–85) and refined with the assistance of his colleague Beno Gutenberg. The scale was the result of eight years of research, and was introduced in 1935 originally to detect seismic tremors around the Californian fault lines. Each point on the scale represents a ten-fold increase in magnitude. The most powerful earthquake, measuring 8.6, was recorded in Ecuador in 1906. A prolonged quake in 1556 was responsible for the greatest number of recorded fatalities, when 830,000 people perished in Shanxi province in China.

Rickenbacker

Trademark name for a range of electric guitars, popularized by groups including the Beatles and the Byrds. Swiss-born toolmaker Adolph Rickenbacker (1887–1976) and his colleague George Beauchamp are widely credited with introducing the first commercially produced electric guitars in 1930. The early models made by the pair's Electro String Instrument Company featured a microphone placed at the rear of a conventional acoustic guitar and hooked up to a loudspeaker. The company began making solid-bodied instruments following its sale to a Californian businessman in 1954. The twelve-string version from the 1960s introduced the distinctive 'jangling' sound that characterizes *A Hard Day's Night* and the Byrds' version of *Mr Tambourine Man*.

Rip van Winkle

One who oversleeps, a person who cannot keep up with the times, taken from the story published in Washington Irving's *The Sketch Book of Geoffrey Crayon, Gent* (1819). The good-natured Rip loses his way in the Catskill Mountains and settles down for a nap. He awakens to discover his gun has rusted and his dog missing. On returning to town he realizes that he has slept for twenty years and events such as the American War of Independence have passed him by completely.

Ritzy

Opulent, classy. Swiss hotelier and restaurateur César Ritz (1850–1918) established the luxurious Ritz Hotels in Paris and London. Irving Berlin's 1929 song *Putting on the Ritz,* adopted a popular euphemism for a display of opulence and glamour, further enhancing the hotels' reputation. The same phrase is sometimes turned upside-down to mean a haughty display of superiority.

Robin Hood

Charitable or honourable thief; benefactor of the poor. The legendary hero of Sherwood Forest and the tormentor of the greedy Sheriff of Nottingham 'robbed from the rich to give to the poor'. The first recorded version of his story appeared in 1377 and innumerable historically shaky film and television interpretations have ensured that his legend survives. Robin's true identity remains hotly contested; the most popular candidate is Robert Fitzooth, the Earl of Huntingdon.

Robinson Crusoe

Isolated person, from the shipwrecked hero of Daniel Defoe's novel of the same name (1719) and its two sequels. Crusoe is at first a stubborn and impatient character but over time shows resourcefulness and increasingly relies on faith to overcome his circumstances. He happily remains on the island, situated somewhere in the West Indies, for twenty-four years before being found by a passing ship. The story is based on the true-life adventures of Scottish buccaneer Alexander Selkirk (1676–1721), who quarrelled with his captain and in 1704 was put ashore at his insistence on the uninhabited island of Juan Fernández in the South Pacific. He survived for four years until his rescue and served out his final days as a naval lieutenant.

Rolls-Royce

High quality. The experimental motor cars built by engineer and electric crane manufacturer Sir Frederick Henry Royce (1863–1933) came to the attention of the aristocratic automobile dealer Charles Stewart Rolls (1877–1910). In 1906 they agreed to merge their operations to found Rolls-Royce Ltd, which soon developed a reputation as the makers of the 'best cars in the world' and later aeroplane engines. Ironically, Rolls, a pioneer aviator who became the first man to cross the English Channel twice in one flight, also became the first Englishman to lose his life in a plane crash. Royce was elevated to the peerage and, despite a brush with bankruptcy in the 1970s, the company's name remains a byword for prestige.

Romeo

Romantic lover. The young star-crossed lovers Romeo and Juliet fall for one another in spite of the feud between their two families, the Montagus and Capulets. When Romeo is banished from Verona, Juliet's unsuspecting family promise her in marriage to another but rather than betray her sweetheart, she drinks a potion to feign death. The returning Romeo believes that Juliet has committed suicide and kills himself in remorse. Juliet awakes only to discover the horrible consequences of her actions and she too takes her own life. William Shakespeare's famous play (1594) did much to popularize the story, which was first recorded by the Italian writer Luigi da Porto in 1535.

Rorschach inkblot test

Test devised by Swiss psychiatrist Hermann Rorshach (1884–1922) to help in the diagnosis of psychopathological conditions. Patients are shown ten inkblots and asked to interpret the random patterns. Their responses are supposed to give some indication of their character but the medical fraternity is divided on the test's effectiveness. Rorschach, whose childhood nickname was 'Kleck' or 'inkblot' for his incessant doodling, began experiments on 400 patients in 1918 and the following year was elected president of the Swiss Psychoanalytic Society. The test was adopted for widespread clinical use in 1921.

Rubenesque

Denoting a shapely, larger woman as depicted by Sir Peter Paul Rubens (1577–1640). Like those of his contemporaries, the major civic and ecclesiastical commissions undertaken by the Flemish artist were usually the work of assistants who would follow sketches and plans. Their master would add a flourish here and there. It left Rubens with more time for portrait work and for his other professional pursuit, diplomacy. 'I regard all the world as my country, and I believe I should be welcome everywhere,' he wrote.

Rubik's cube

Fiendishly difficult mathematical puzzle conceived by Hungarian architect and teacher Ernö Rubik (1944–). The six-sided cube, represented by a different colour on each face, divides into twenty-six smaller cubes connected by ball-and-socket joints. The challenge is to return the colours to their original position by rotating the cubes on a pivoting axis. There are billions of permutations but only one solution. The puzzle was patented in 1975 and became a worldwide craze in the early 1980s.

Sabin vaccine

Protective preparation against polio administered orally. Russian-born US virologist Albert Bruce Sabin (1906–1993) pioneered the use of vaccines containing the live virus to help stimulate the generation of antibodies. Previous vaccines made with the dead virus provided only limited protection against disease and patients required regular revaccination. Sabin guessed that what he called the live-attenuated virus would allow the spread of a harmless infection but prevent the development of the disease. His faith was tested in 1957 when Sabin and his family became the first guinea pigs. The results proved conclusive and within four years the new vaccine was commercially available.

Sadism

Sexual gratification derived from inflicting pain upon another. Donatien Alphonse François, Comte de Sade (1740–1814), known as the Marquis de Sade, described in graphic detail a catalogue of sexual depravity in his novels and plays, most of which were written in prison, where he died. The aristocratic Frenchman practised what he preached; following his service in the Seven Years' War, de Sade was imprisoned for inflicting sexual abuse on prostitutes but returned to his debauched ways upon his release. Repeatedly he was thrown into jail and narrowly escaped two death sentences. The forensic nature of his material, which appalled Revolutionary France, won academic plaudits throughout the twentieth century; de Sade is often said to have paved the way for Freud and movements such as existentialism.

Sally Lunn

Teacakes made from yeast dough that, it is said, were first baked in Bath in the eighteenth century by a pastry cook of the same name. John Ayto's *A Gourmet's Guide* suggests the name in fact derives from the French *soleil lune* 'sun and moon' cake. In the southern US, Sally Lunn is the name given to soda bread.

Salmonella

Bacteria which causes typhoid and remains the most common form of food poisioning in humans was identified by US veterinary pathologist Daniel Elmer Salmon (1850–1914). All foods of animal origin are susceptible to infection and most varieties of the disease can be eliminated by heating food for fifteen minutes at 60°C. Salmon was a US Agriculture Department investigator before becoming the head of the Bureau of Animal Investigation, where he instituted safeguards against contaminated meat.

Sam Browne

The leather pistol belt worn over the shoulder was an essential part of the British officer's uniform until 1939. It

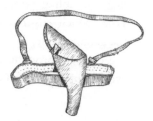

was invented by General Sir Samuel James Browne (1824–1901) who lost his left arm in the Indian mutiny and was awarded the Victoria Cross in 1861 for his gallantry.

Samson

An uncommonly strong man, in reference to the judge of ancient Israel whose story is told in the Old Testament. The Philistines employed the seductress Delilah to discover the secret of Samson's great strength. His fate was sealed when he confided that his hair possessed special powers; Delilah cut it off and delivered Samson into the hands of the enemy. Chained to the pillars of the temple, he prayed for divine intervention. Samson's strength was restored and he pulled the temple down, killing 3,000 people.

Sandwich

Slices of bread with filling. It is ironic that the most common and innocuous eponym derives from the most hated figure in eighteenth-century politics. John Montagu, 4th Earl of Sandwich (1718–92), was accused of bribery and corruption while First Lord of the Admiralty and was blamed for the ill-preparedness of the navy at the time of French aggression and the American Revolution (the bottom literally fell out of one vessel, the *Royal George*, while still in port). His darkest hour came in 1763 when he led the prosecution of his former friend, John Wilkes, altering documents to ensure incrimination. Yet it was a marathon all-night gambling session, in between political appointments in 1762, which ensured his place in history. Unwilling to leave the gaming table, His Lordship called for some sliced meat and bread to be brought to him, changing the face of cuisine for ever. Captain James Cook repaid Sandwich's patronage of his expeditions by giving his name to an outcrop in the Pacific. The **Sandwich Islands** later became known as Hawaii.

Sapphism

Female homosexuality. Sappho remains the most famous of the women poets who resided on the isle of Lesbos in the Aegean Sea in the seventh century BC. One of her works is still intact, an address to Aphrodite; of the rest only fragments remain. Sappho's poems celebrate the love of a woman for a girl. Some scholars believe she was a mentor or teacher to her female audience.

Saturn

The sixth planet from the sun, orbiting between Jupiter and Uranus, and distinguished by its three rings consisting of icy particles. Saturn was the all-powerful Roman god of time who taught basic agricultural and social skills to mortals. He was eventually deposed by his son, Jupiter, one of three children he had chosen not to devour (the others were Neptune and Pluto). We still honour Saturn on the day the Romans dedicated to him, **Saturday**, and sometimes refer to debauched proceedings as **Saturnalia**, after the annual Roman revelries in December when criminals were exempted from punishment and slaves were allowed to mock their masters. A person with a **saturnine** disposition is moody or gloomy; Saturn was sometimes connected with the underworld and is considered by astrologers to be a bad planet.

Saxophone

Brass wind instrument devised by Antoine Joseph (known as Adolphe) Sax (1814–94), a Belgian instrument-maker and inventor. The saxophone, patented in Paris in 1846, was one of a family of instruments which he invented, including the Saxhorn and the Sax-Tromba. The shrewd Sax courted influential patrons in French music, such as Berlioz, and in the army, ensuring at one stage that his inventions alone were played by French military bands. Alas, he did not possess a head for figures and Sax's fortune declined in later years.

Scrooge

Miser. Ebenezer Scrooge was the penny-pinching anti-hero of Charles Dickens' (*see* **Dickensian**) *A Christmas Carol* (1843) who was shown the error of his miserly ways by the ghosts of Christmas Past, Present and Yet to Come.

Sequoia

Genus of tall, coniferous tree native to North America. Sequoiah or Sequoya (1770–1843) was a mixed-race native American who invented a method of transcribing the Cherokee language. He was born in Tennessee, the son of a British merchant and a Cherokee woman and took the name George Guess later in life, after his father. His name is also perpetuated in the Sequoia National Park in California, where ancient giant sequoias still thrive.

Shrapnel

Fragments of high-explosive shells or bombs. Royal Artillery lieutenant Henry Shrapnel (1761–1842) spent much of his life and his own savings devising a hollow bomb capable of distributing lead pellets and grapeshot across a wide area while in flight. His invention, first used in battle in the British attack on Surinam in 1804, became known as the shrapnel shell and was employed to great effect at Waterloo. Its enthusiastic advocates included the Duke of Wellington but, alas, Shrapnel's only reward was a meagre pension and eventual promotion to the rank of lieutenant-general. In 1837 a grateful George IV sought to honour Shrapnel for services to his country but the monarch died that same year and the impetus was lost. Shrapnel died a disappointed man. The use of the word shrapnel for shell fragments was in common usage by World War II.

Shylock

Mean-hearted person who demands greater payment than is fair for a transaction. The Jewish moneylender in William Shakespeare's *Merchant of Venice* (1595) demanded a pound of flesh as collateral for a loan to Antonio. When Antonio could not repay the loan, Shylock demanded full payment.

Sideburns

Unshaven side-whiskers worn below the ear were originally called burnsides, after Ambrose Everett Burnside (1824–81), a Union general in the Civil War, whose huge mutton chops popularized the look in the US. The name was transposed soon after. Burnside suffered mixed fortunes during the war; he triumphantly routed the Confederates at Knoxville, Tennessee, but incurred heavy losses in Virginia and was forced to resign. His military career at an end, the General entered politics, becoming Governor of Rhode Island and subsequently serving as a senator.

Silhouette

Outline of an object or person taken from their shadow; similar portraits painted or cut out of black card. Étienne de Silhouette (1709–67), who served a brief tenure as France's Finance Minister, was derided by the nobility for being a mere 'shadow' of a politician; he is also thought to have invented the distinctive style of portraiture which grew in popularity throughout the eighteenth and nineteenth centuries.

Singer sewing machine

Isaac Singer (1811–76) popularized the sewing machine, in turn becoming the first man to spend more than one million dollars a year on advertising, but it was not his invention by any means. That distinction belongs to an English cabinet-maker, Thomas Saint, who patented his contraption in 1790, though there is no evidence the design ever left the drawing board. The principle impediment in the way of the machine's early developers was the fear of job losses. A French tailor, Barthelemy Thimonnier, patented his own design in 1830, which could sew 200 stitches in one minute, compared to a seamster's thirty. Custom flowed until Parisian hand-tailors saw that their livelihood was in danger; they subsequently threatened Thimonnier's life and wrecked his shop. Similar reprisals stopped an American inventor, Walter Hunt, from marketing his invention several years later. Singer's predominance had its genesis in the 1840s, when a sewing machine invented by an American mechanic, Elias Howe, endured uninterested and unscrupulous backers both in the US and Britain. Howe went to court, winning substantial damages from other manufacturers who had infringed his patents.

Among them was Isaac Singer, who suggested all patents should be pooled. Howe drew royalties from all subsequent sales, but it was Singer who won fame and fortune.

Solomon, wisdom of

The son of King David, Soloman (d. *c.* 930 BC) was the last king of a united Israel and noted for his wisdom. But he was also a harsh ruler; he instituted a heavy taxation regime and forced labour. To please his harem of 700 wives and 300 concubines he allowed the worship of idols. Solomon's policies contributed to the break up of the kingdom on his death.

Sousaphone

Large, brass wind instrument devised by C.G. Conn in 1899 expressly for John Philip Sousa (1854-1932), the US bandleader and composer of military marches. The most American of composers was the son of a Portuguese father and a Bavarian mother. After playing the violin in a dance band in his teenage years, Sousa rose to prominence as the leader of the US Marine Corps band and became known as 'the March King', touring his own band internationally. His compositions included suites for orchestra and operettas but he is remembered chiefly for his one hundred marches, including *Stars and Stripes Forever* (1897) and *Liberty Bell* (1893), which has since been immortalized as the *Monty Python* theme tune.

Spencer

Women's undergarment or tight-fitting sweater, usually made of wool. Originally a spencer was a waist-length fitted jacket, as worn by George John, 2nd Earl Spencer (1758–1834), who is said to have started the fashion. In the early nineteenth-century women adopted the mode of dress, styling the jackets in wool or silk to be worn with the high-waisted skirts of the day. Spencer was a Whig politician and statesman who, as First Lord of the Admiralty, presided over the British Navy at the time of its greatest strength. It was Spencer who saw the potential of Horatio Nelson and ensured his command of the heroic Battle of the Nile against Napoleon's fleet in 1798. His descendants include Winston Churchill. The current earl is the brother of the Princess of Wales.

Sphinx

An enigmatic person. The Theban monster of Greek mythology bore the head of a woman and the winged body of a lion. She would lie in wait, posing riddles to passersby, devouring those who answered incorrectly. Oedipus was asked 'What walks on four legs in the morning, on two in the afternoon and on three in the evening?' The answer he gave was 'a man' – who crawls on all fours as an infant and is supported by a stick in old age. The sphinx was so horrified at the thought of being outwitted that she threw herself off a cliff. The Egyptian sphinx at Giza bears a lion's body and a pharoah's head to symbolize majesty.

Spinet

Small stringed musical instrument resembling a harpsichord. Giovanni Spinetti was a Venetian instrument-maker who was fashioning spinets as early as 1503 and is considered their inventor. It is also suggested that because the strings were plucked like a harpsichord's, the name derives from *spina*, the Italian for thorn.

Spinets were popular in eighteenth-century England and at one time the name was applied to all similar instruments. However, unlike the harpsichord, each string on the spinet plays only one note.

Spoonerisms

An Oxford don, the Reverend William Archibald Spooner (1844–1930), gave his name to a slip of the tongue by which syllables of certain words are transposed, often with comic results. 'The Lord is a shoving leopard' is an oft-quoted example. Yet Spooner was far from the doddering fool of popular myth and his own lapses into Spoonerisms were by all accounts occasional. Despite poor eyesight (he was albino), the reverend published a translation of the *Histories of Tacitus* (1891) and wrote several historical biographies.

Stanley knife

Trademark name for a knife with a retractable blade which can be replaced when blunt; more commonly any knife of similar design. Connecticut entrepreneur Frederick T. Stanley founded a factory to manufacture wrought-iron bolts, handles and hinges in 1843, eventually merging with the woodworking-tools business of his prosperous cousin, Henry (who originated the familiar notched rectangle logo). The stainless-steel knife was introduced in the 1940s and is produced in the UK at the company's hand-tools works in Sheffield.

St Bernard

Rescue dog trained as a pathfinder by the canons of the alpine hospice established by St Bernard of Aosta (d. 1081). The heavy, muscular dogs were celebrated for aiding travellers along the snowbound St Bernard Pass, between Switzerland and Italy. St Bernard was a familiar figure in the remote region and was named patron saint of mountain climbers in 1923.

Sten gun

The first mass-produced British sub-machine gun, rapidly adopted for use in 1940 during the darkest days of World War II. The pared-down weapon took its name from the location of the factory where it was produced and the initials of its designers, Major R.V. Shepherd and H.J. Turpin, two members of the Small Arms Group at the Royal Small Arms Factory at Enfield, in north London. But the Sten gun ran into problems in the field where dirt caught in the magazine would cause the weapon to seize up. Its cousin, the **Bren gun**, a light machine gun introduced in 1937, which was designed in Brno, Moravia, and manufactured at Enfield, proved far more reliable.

Stentorian

Distinctly loud voice. Stentor was a Thracian herald in the Trojan war who, according to Homer's *Iliad*, had a voice as loud as fifty men. He was killed by the messenger of the gods, Hermes, whom he had challenged to a shouting match.

Stetson

Men's slouch hat worn in the American West, an essential accessory for cowboys. The felt headgear with the broad brim and high crown was made by John Batterson Stetson

(1830–1906), a New Jersey hatmaker. Stetson had his grounding in the trade in the family hat-making business and opened his own factory in Philadelphia in 1865. The famous cowboy hat is also sometimes called a John B.

Stonewall

To obstruct. The Confederate General Thomas Jonathan 'Stonewall' Jackson (1824–63) acquired his nickname at the First Battle of Bull Run in 1861. The line of troops, led by Jackson 'standing like a stone wall', successfully withheld the numerically superior enemy against overwhelming odds. Like the French Marquis de Martinet two hundred years before, the general was accidentally shot by his own men at the Battle of Chancellorville. In the game of cricket, the verb 'to stonewall' has been applied since the 1880s to batsmen who play on the defensive.

St Vitus's dance

Nervous disorder prevalent in children which is characterized by involuntary spasms, now called Sydenham's chorea. The best cure is rest. A curious epidemic of excitable dancing was recorded in Germany in the Middle Ages. Sufferers travelled to the chapels of the third-century Italian saint (d. *c.* 303) where they believed his spirit could provide a cure. The two conditions are unconnected. St Vitus became the patron saint of people suffering from nervous conditions and later, actors and dancers.

Svengali

A mentor, one who exercises influence over another through mystical powers or psychological control. Svengali was a musician who exerted a hypnotic influence over the eponymous heroine of the novel *Trilby* (1894) by George du Maurier. With her mentor's help, Trilby went on to become a superb singer. Du Maurier based the character on his friend Felix Moscheles, an artist and amateur mesmerist.

Sweet Fanny Adams

Nothing at all. The grisly murder and dismemberment of eight-year-old Fanny Adams (1859–67) at Hampshire and the subsequent trial mesmerized (*see* **mesmerize**) Victorian England. A crowd of 5,000 people gathered to watch the killer, Frederick Baker, swing from the gallows. About that time the Royal Navy began serving tinned mutton on board ships. It henceforth became a sick joke among sailors to swear blind that they had found one of sweet Fanny Adams's buttons in the stew. Her name became a euphemism for any equally vacuous assertions.

Syphilis

Venereal disease that takes its name from *Syphilis sive Morbus Gallicus* (1530), a poem by the Veronese astronomer, physicist and poet Girolamo Fracastoro (1483–1553). The mournful verse tells the story of the death from the pox of the title character, a shepherd, who displeased the gods. The name is derived from Sypilus, the elder son of Niobe, the Greek goddess of maternal sorrow whose fourteen children were all killed by a jealous rival.

Tantalize

To tease by promising something and then failing to deliver. The nymph Tantalus, a son of Zeus, was banished to the Underworld for excessive self-pride. All food and drink were placed out of reach and when he did extend his arm to grasp the fruit of a tree, the branch withdrew even further away. The reasons for his punishment differ, depending on the telling of the story. He is variously accused of having stolen the nectar of the gods and introducing it to humans and of cooking his son to serve as a meal to the gods.

Tantony pig

The runt of the litter. Pigs belonging to the Order of Hospitallers of St Anthony in the Middle Ages were allowed to run freely in the streets, protected from disease, it was thought, by the bells round their necks. St Anthony of Egypt (AD 251–356) began the Christian tradition of monasticism with St Paul the Hermit. In later iconography he is accompanied by a pig and depicted carrying a small church bell, which also came to bear the name Tantony.

Tarmac

Stone or gravel road paving, latterly covered with asphalt or tar. Scottish engineer John Loudon McAdam (1756–1836) resolved to do something about the poor state of the roads surrounding his Ayrshire estate. In Cornwall he carried out his experiments with government patronage, making roads sturdier by raising them above the ground; this way water could drain away adequately. He also covered them with crushed rocks, stones and a coating of gravel. McAdam's methods, which came to be known as **macadamization**, brought improvements in transport and commerce and were rapidly adopted in Britain and the US. **Tarmacadam** added a surface coating of tar and the name 'Tarmac' was registered as a trademark in the US in 1903.

Tawdry

Cheap, showy and of poor quality. Poor St Audrey (c. AD 630–679)! How did the name of a godly East Anglian monarch come to signify anything inferior or of little value? In fact, the word comes from the tatty lace and cheap jewellery that was sold at the Cambridgeshire fair held annually on her feast day in October. The virginal Audrey remained chaste throughout two marriages and gave up her noble life for an ascetic existence, founding a monastery on the Isle of Ely. When she developed a tumour on her neck, a symptom of the plague, she took it as divine retribution for wearing necklaces in her youth. Etheldreda, as she was known, was one of the most popular of the early Anglo-Saxon saints.

Teddy bear

US president Theodore Roosevelt (1858–1919), known universally as 'Teddy' cultivated a reputation as an outdoorsman, hunting wild creatures including bears. But according to one story, probably dubious, it is said that while out hunting one day the rugged statesman came across a lone bear club, aimed his rifle but could not bring himself to pull the trigger. The toys came onto the market soon after Roosevelt became president in 1901 and the name was swiftly adopted. Roosevelt was the first American to win the Nobel peace prize for his role as mediator in the war between Russia and Japan.

Tesla coil

Transformer used in electrical equipment such as television sets, which require high voltages of electric current at high frequencies. Croatian-born US electrical engineer and physicist Nikola Tesla (1856–1943) was a leading figure in the battle to deliver electricity to the home. He found a practical way to harness alternating current, or AC, and teamed up with George Westinghouse to exploit his discovery. Their method dealt a blow to Tesla's former boss, Thomas Alva Edison, whose fortune was invested in direct current, or DC. The eccentric inventor, who claimed he had communicated with outer space, also gives his name to the **tesla**, a unit measuring the density of magnetic flux, identified by the symbol 'T'.

Thespian

An actor, specifically a tragedian. According to legend, the poet Thespis presented the first Greek tragedies in Athens around 536 BC. Until that time performances were given by a chorus. Thespis allowed individual members to play specific characters, laying the foundations for contemporary dramatic art.

Thursday

Fifth day of the week that honours Thor, the Norse god of thunder, whose counterparts are also recalled in the German and French names for Thursday. The Teutonic Donar gives us *Donnerstag*; in Roman mythology Jove was responsible for thunder, hence *jeudi*. Thor possessed great physical strength and carried a magic hammer that created thunder and lightening when thrown.

Tommy

British private soldier. In the early nineteenth century, compulsory manuals in which soldiers were to note their service records came with specimen forms bearing the name Thomas Atkins. When a military paper was submitted to the Duke of Wellington suggesting a typical name for a private, he apparently crossed out the entry and substituted the name of a veteran of his old regiment. Private Thomas Atkins had served with the Iron Duke during the retreat from Antwerp in 1794. An original paybook with Atkins's name at the top of the page and the date 24.6.1815 at the bottom rests in the collection of the Royal Army Military College Historical Museum at Aldershot.

Tommy gun

Short-barrelled sub-machine gun, initially marketed as a weapon for police but which found greater popularity among Depression-era gangsters and the military. US Army ordnance officer John Tagliaferro Thompson (1860–1940) spent much of his life trying to devise the ideal automatic rifle. He bought a patent for such a weapon from a naval officer, John Blish, and in 1919 engineers at Thompson's own Auto-Ordnance Company produced the first sub-machine gun, the Trench Broom. It found little commercial success until after Thompson's death when the improved Thompson M1928A1, the Tommy gun, was adopted for use by US marines in World War II.

Tom Thumb

The tiny hero of children's stories no larger than a thumb made his first appearance in English literature in 1579. The character was personified by Charles Sherwood Stratton (1838–83), an American dwarf who performed in the travelling shows of the impresario Phineas Taylor Barnum. 'General Tom Thumb', as Stratton was dubbed, stood three feet four inches tall and was one of Barnum's most popular exhibits.

Topsy

To 'grow like Topsy' is to develop or multiply without any apparent effort. Ignorant of her parentage, Topsy was a mischievous black girl who claimed to have 'just growed' in *Uncle Tom's Cabin* (1852), by US novelist Harriet Beecher Stowe.

Trilby

Men's felt hat with an indented crown, named after the eponymous heroine of George du Maurier's 1894 novel. A young artists' model, Trilby O'Ferrall, rises to fame as a singer under the influence of the mysterious musician Svengali (*see* **Svengali**). But when her mentor dies of a heart attack she loses her ability to sing. Trilby too falls ill and follows Svengali to the grave.

Tuesday

Third day of the week, named after the Norse god Tiu or Tyr, who corresponds with the Teutonic Tiwaz and the Roman Mars (in French, Tuesday is *mardi*). Tiu is the younger brother of Thor (Thursday). He lost a hand while chained to Fenrir, a wolf belonging to Loki, the spirit of evil.

Tupperware

Proprietary name for a range of plastic kitchenware with airtight lids. In 1942 Massachusetts chemist Earl Tupper (1907–83) developed a method of injection-moulding polyethylene, an unbreakable plastic developed by ICI. He established Tupper Plastics and promoted the containers not in stores but at Tupperware parties, in-home demonstrations for neighbourhood housewives. Tupper sold his company to Rexall Drug in 1952 and the company moved its manufacturing plant to Florida. By the 1980s, Tupper's plastic goods were considered design classics and a permanent collection was established at the Museum of Modern Art in New York.

$\mathcal{U}$

Uncle Tom

Black person who is servile to the white community or actively assimilationist. The black slave of Harriet Beecher Stowe's novel *Uncle Tom's Cabin, or, Life Among the Lowly* (1852) earned the emnity of later generations of African Americans for his accepting attitude to his master, the cruel Simon Legree. Some academics have attempted to link the passive suffering of the book's title character to the life of Christ. Uncle Tom was apparently based on the story of a real-life slave, Josiah Henson.

Uranus

Seventh planet from the sun and the first planet to be discovered by telescope. It was first sighted by Sir William Herschel from his garden in Bath in 1781 and originally named *Georgium Sidus* after George III. The planet has a mass fifteen times that of the earth and a surface temperature of a brisk -240°C. Uranus is the Greek god of heaven or the sky. He fathered eighteen children in all, including the Titans, which rather wore out his exhausted wife, Gaia (earth). Deciding enough was enough, she pleaded for assistance from her sons. Chronus (time) alone took a scythe and cut off his father's testicles.

Uzi gun

The Arab-Israeli Wars of 1948–9 prompted Israel army officer Major Uziel Gal to design a simple sub-machine gun, based on other guns then in use in the region and easy to manufacture from stamped metal. The compact Uzi, with the magazine contained in the pistol grip, was introduced in 1952 and adopted by the Israeli forces. Other countries including Germany and Iran were also to use the weapon.

Venereal

Once used to denote lust, the adjective has come to be associated solely with sexually transmitted diseases. The word derives from the name of Venus, the Roman goddess of love (whose Greek equivalent is Aphrodite). 'Venus's curse' was nineteenth-century slang for gonorrhea.

Venn diagram

A series of overlapping circles, in which the intersecting areas represent the relationship between different groups. English mathematician and cleric, John Venn (1834–1923) devised the diagrams as a tool to explain logical propositions. Charles Lutwidge Dodgson, who as Lewis Carroll found fame as the author of the *Alice in Wonderland* stories, later refined Venn's ideas.

Vestal

Denoting chastity and purity. The six vestal virgins guarded the sacred flame at the temple of the goddess Vesta in Rome. The Romans believed the flame, brought from Troy, protected the city and had to remain alight at all costs. The vestals began their training at the age of ten and altogether spent thirty years in the service of the temple. Anyone who broke the vow of chastity was sentenced to death.

Volt

Electrical unit. Alessandro Volta (1745–1827) built the first battery, producing electricity by combining different metals in a damp atmosphere. Other scientists made improvements yet today's batteries follow the same basic design. Thankfully the original name didn't stick: the Voltaic pile.

Walter Mitty

Someone who withdraws into a fantasy world rather than face reality. *The Secret Life of Walter Mitty* (1939) by US humorist James Thurber told the story of a meek husband who escaped his drab existence by dreaming up heroic fantasies. His nagging wife was none the wiser.

Wankel rotary engine

Compact automobile engine invented by German engineer Felix Wankel (1902–88) in which an orbiting rotor replaces moving pistons. The rotary engine was greeted with enthusiasm by the motor industry upon its introduction in 1957 – it was adopted briefly by Mazda and Citroën – but it never succeeded in replacing the internal combustion engine. It proved to be more efficient on the drawing board than in practice, at a time when the price of oil was beginning its heady rise and manufacturers became reluctant to invest in its continued development.

Watt

Unit of electricity, equivalent to one joule per second. Scottish engineer James Watt (1736–1819) refined the design of the steam-powered piston engine. By adding a separate condensing system the engine was able to retain much more heat, thus reducing fuel consumption. Watt's invention of 1765 fuelled the industrial revolution: it became the principal source of power for Britain's burgeoning textile mills. Little remembered is Watt's role with his colleague William Murdoch in pioneering the pneumatic dispatch tube, so beloved by American industry in the mid-twentieth century.

Wedgwood

Elegant pottery of neo-classical design made by Staffordshire potter Josiah Wedgwood (1730–95) and his followers. Wedgwood conducted meticulous experiments in order to learn more about the properties of glazes. His patient work led most notably to the invention of Jasper Ware, which imitated the style of Greco-Roman pieces. Wedgwood's innovative stoneware and earthenware designs earned him the patronage of the royal houses of Europe. He was a vocal supporter of the American Revolution and the grandfather of Charles Darwin (*see* **Darwinism**).

Wednesday

Fourth day of the week, dedicated to Odin (Woden, in later Germanic myth), the Norse deity and hero of Scandanavian warriors. Odin was the eldest son of Thor, whose legend eventually displaced that of his father. He traded one of his eyes for the gift of wisdom and was accompanied at all times by two ravens. He is equated with the Roman messenger of the gods Mercury, hence the French name for Wednesday, *mercredi*. Odin's wife Freya gives her name to Friday (*see* **Friday**).

Wellington

Originally men's leather riding boots covering the knee introduced in the early nineteenth century; later, shorter boots worn under the trousers; today **wellies** are rubber or synthetic boots worn in inclement weather. Arthur Wellesley, the 1st Duke of Wellington (1769-1852), hero of Waterloo and later Prime Minister, introduced or inspired other articles of clothing including the Wellington coat, hat and trousers. Wellington may have been a skillful military tactician but he had such an intemperate disposition even his friends were compelled to admit 'he was not an amiable man'; he once described his own troops as 'the scum of the earth, enlisted for drink'. When his opposition to parliamentary reform threatened to incite rioting on the streets of London, Wellington ordered metal shutters to be fitted to the windows of his home, thus earning him the nickname the Iron Duke. A species of sequoia tree native to North America, *sequoia giganteum*, was named **Wellingtonia** in his honour.

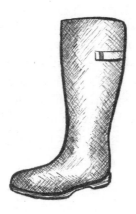

Wendy house

Girls' playhouse named after the matriarchal Wendy Moira Angela Darling, who, with her siblings, was enlisted by J.M. Barrie's *Peter Pan: or The Boy Who Would Not Grow Up* to rescue the Lost Boys from the clutches of the evil Captain Hook.

Williams pear

Juicy variety, which ripens in September, the correct title of which is the Williams Bon Chrétien pear. In the eighteenth century a certain Mr Williams, a nurseryman from Turnham Green, distributed the fruit in England; it was supposedly introduced into France three hundred years earlier by St François hence its French name, which means 'good Christian'. The trees crossed the Atlantic with Captain Thomas Brewer, who grew the pears on his property in Dorchester, Massachusetts. A merchant, Enoch Bartlett (1779–1860), bought Brewer's farm and popularized the fruit under his own name in North America, where it is still known as the **Bartlett pear**.

Winchester rifle

Trademark repeating rifle. In 1855 US shirt manufacturer Oliver Winchester (1810-80) purchased a failed arms company in which he had made an investment. Despite poor sales to the Union Army during the Civil War, Winchester turned instead to the civilian market among whom the firm's redesigned rifles sold well. An automatic rifle designed and built by the Winchester company was adopted for use by US Army supply troops in World War II; it is still in widespread use.

Windsor knot

Large loose knot in a necktie, after the fashion of Prince Edward, the Duke of Windsor (1894–1972), formerly Edward VIII. Americans once believed the Duke wore a style of neckwear known as 'God's tie'. His upper-class vowels obviously lost something in the translation; it was, in fact, the Guard's tie that the former monarch wore. Edward abdicated from the throne in 1936 to marry the American divorcee, Wallis Warfield Simpson.

Wisteria

Genus of climbing plants with racemes of blue, purple or white flowers, native to the US, China and Japan; a bluish-lilac colour. Caspar Wistar (1761–1818) was Professor of Anatomy at Pennsylvania University. Upon his death, his friend and colleague the English-born Thomas Nuttall christened the genus Wistaria. But over the next fifty years few people took any notice. The name was nearly universally misspelled; wysteria, westeria and finally the accepted spelling today, wisteria. The Oxford English Dictionary concedes either version – wisteria or wistaria – is accepted.

Wurlitzer organ

The 'Mighty Wurlitzer' theatre organ remains the world's best-selling pipe organ. It was originally called the 'Unit Orchestra' and was a familiar sight in picture palaces in the golden age of silent cinema. When his Ohio music store was unable to meet the demand for musical instruments, German-born Rudolph Wurlitzer (1831–1914) founded the family firm of instrument-makers. The company bought an organ works in New York in 1910 and production of the 'Mighty Wurlitzer' began thereafter.

Yahoo

Boor; an exclamation. Originally a brutish race who embodied the worst vices of humans, in Jonathan Swift's *Gulliver's Travels* (1726).

Yale lock

Trademark name for locks, including a type of pin-tumbler lock devised by New England inventor Linnus Yale (1821–88). An artist, Yale followed in his father's footsteps and manufactured locks for banks. He adapted techniques first used in ancient Egypt to develop the lock with the revolving barrel. Yale died that same year.

Zeppelin

Type of airship containing a helium gas cell within a lightweight metal frame. Pioneer Ferdinand, Count von Zeppelin (1838–1917), built his first airship in 1898. Larger craft for passenger voyages soon followed. The Graf Zeppelin made 144 transatlantic trips but the craft were taken out of service after the world's largest airship, the Hindenberg, caught fire in the US in 1937, killing thirty-five people.

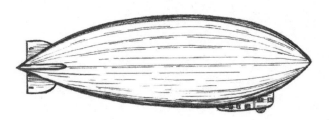